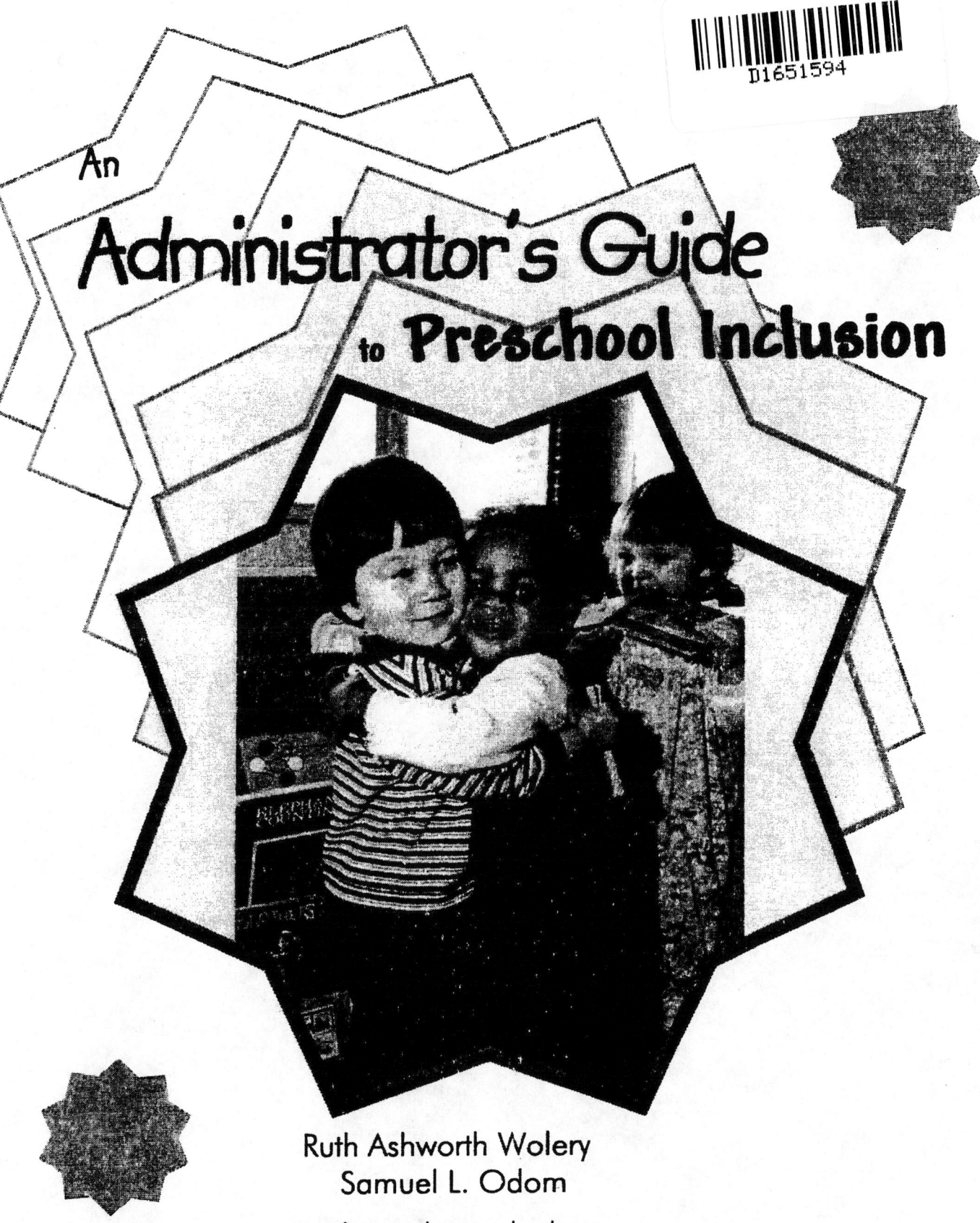

An Administrator's Guide to Preschool Inclusion

Ruth Ashworth Wolery
Samuel L. Odom

with contributions by the
Early Childhood Research Institute on Inclusion

An Administrator's Guide to Preschool Inclusion

Ruth Ashworth Wolery
Samuel L. Odom

with

Contributions from ECRII Investigators and Staff

Paula H. Beckman

Marci J. Hanson

Eva Horn

Susan Janko

Kristine J. Kuczynski

Phyllis Levinsen

Shouming Li

Joan Lieber

Jules Marquart

Susan Sandall

Ilene Schwartz

EARLY CHILDHOOD RESEARCH INSTITUTE ON INCLUSION (ECRII)

For more information about the institute, please visit our website at
www.fpg.unc.edu/~ecrii

Please cite publication as:

Wolery, R. A., & Odom, S. L. (2000). *An administrator's guide to pre-school inclusion*. Chapel Hill: University of North Carolina, FPG Child Development Center, Early Childhood Research Institute on Inclusion.

Design by Kristine J. Kuczynski

Photography by Don Trull and Pat Wesley
Children from the Frank Porter Graham Child Care Center

For additional information about the content of this product, contact

Samuel L. Odom   Ruth A. Wolery
Indiana University   Vanderbilt University
School of Education   Peabody College of Education
201 North Rose Street   21st Avenue South, Box 321
Bloomington, IN 47405-1006   Nashville, TN 37203

To order additional copies,
contact the FPG Publications Office
Phone: (919) 966-4221
Fax: (919) 966-0862
Email: pubs@mail.fpg.unc.edu

Support for *An Administrator's Guide to Preschool Inclusion*
was provided in part by funds from the
Office of Special Education Programs and the Office of Educational
Research and Improvement, U. S. Department of Education,
Grant #HC2K40004.

Table of Contents

An Administrator's Guide

Introduction

An Administrator's Guide

For many administrators and educators working in early childhood programs, inclusion is filled with complex and puzzling issues. Administrators hold a powerful role in creating and maintaining inclusive classrooms for young children. Over the past 5 years, we have talked with many administrators who set program policy. These administrators exert key influences over whether or not inclusive classrooms exist, and how successful the programs are for children, teachers, and families. We have learned a lot about how inclusion works and the roles of administrators and policymakers. We have also learned that although administrators' roles are often quite different, they have very similar concerns and frustrations.

In our interviews with administrators and policy makers across the country, we have searched for answers to many questions. What is inclusion? Does it look the same in various places? How do children with disabilities and families gain access to classrooms with typically developing children? How does one recognize quality in inclusive programs? How do administrators help staff work together in these programs? What training is necessary for staff? How much do inclusive programs cost and how does one finance them? How do administrators respond to the desires, wishes, and dreams of the parents and the requirements of the law? How can one change a system that has been providing noninclusive class placements for children since the early 1990s or before? Although there are no definitive answers that apply to every situation, our work with the Early Childhood Research Institute on Inclusion (ECRII) has revealed some of the ways in which administrators and policy makers have successfully addressed these questions.

As researchers with the Early Childhood Research Institute on Inclusion, we have explored the ideas and conditions that characterize preschool inclusion. We have conducted a comprehensive national study of preschool inclusion, funded by the U.S. Department of Education and carried out at five universities: San Francisco State University, the University of

ECRII Administrators' Guide

Maryland, the University of North Carolina, the University of Washington, and Vanderbilt University. This guide is based on the information we gathered from 16 preschool programs serving 112 children with a wide range of disabilities. The programs were located in urban, suburban, and rural communities across the country and included culturally diverse children and adult participants. The 16 programs illustrate the various ways in which young children with disabilities can be included into early childhood settings. ECRII researchers tried to describe and learn about inclusion from those who create and use classrooms and programs—namely, children with and without disabilities, their families, teachers, administrators, and policymakers.

The purpose of this guide is to address some of the issues raised by the administrators of these inclusive settings. We discuss the barriers and roadblocks these administrators encountered as they set up inclusive programs and then worked to keep them going successfully. We present practical strategies that emerged from our work, and we also draw upon the larger literature and work of others. In places, we introduce some of the people who, through their stories and experiences, illustrate how to make high quality early childhood inclusion a reality.

This guide is for administrators who are responsible for setting up, monitoring, supporting, and maintaining inclusive programs for preschool children with and without disabilities. These administrators may be special education directors in public school systems, coordinators for early childhood services, building principals in elementary schools, directors or special needs coordinators in Head Start programs, and, possibly, directors of preschools and child care programs in the community. Although our work, and the focus of this guide, is on programs for 3- to 5-year old children, inclusive programs certainly extend to the many natural environments that exist for toddlers and infants in group settings. Many of the suggestions and ideas offered in this book can also be applied to this age range.

The ECRII investigators are deeply grateful to the administrators and staff of the 16 programs where we conducted our research. We spent many hours in these programs observing children, talking to adults, reviewing records, and learning about inclusion. We also acknowledge the parents who participated in our interviews and surveys and allowed us to better understand preschool inclusion from the families' perspectives. To these wonderful and forthcoming people we offer our heartfelt thanks.

We also are grateful to a number of colleagues who assisted us in the preparation of this product. From providing us with the early childhood professional's perspective on what should be included in the guide, to fine-tune editing of our early drafts, to facilitating the dissemination efforts, we benefited significantly from the time and expertise of the following individuals: Jennifer Annable, Kathy Baars, Cindy Bagwell, Shelley deFosset, Ann Garfinkle, Linda Higgins, Kathleen Hugo, Donice Pulley, Molly Weston, and Mark Wolery. Finally, we thank two individuals from the U.S. Department of Education who have provided ongoing support for our Early Childhood Research Institute on Inclusion: Gail Houle, from the Office of Special Education Programs, and Naomi Karp, from the Office of Educational Research and Improvement. For their support, we are most appreciative. This manual was produced with funds from the U.S. Department of Education, Grant #HC2K40004.

"Inclusion redefines special education as a resource rather than a place." -School System Administrator

Chapter One

What Is Preschool Inclusion ?

> "We know that inclusion is the push, but the system doesn't have a definite 'this is inclusion and this is not inclusion.' So I think what has happened is that schools have taken on the challenge themselves and many schools have been creative in a variety of ways." -Program Administrator

Inclusion is not just a school issue; it is about participation of children (and older individuals) with disabilities as equal and accepted members of society. This societal value influences how school systems and early childhood programs such as Head Start and community-based child care serve young children with disabilities. The most direct form of influence is through legislation and social policies at the national level. In this chapter, we describe the laws and policies that underlie preschool inclusion, we briefly describe the positions taken on providing services for young children, and we propose a number of features of preschool inclusion that have emerged from our research. But first, we examine how inclusion for preschool children is different from inclusion for older children. These differences sometimes pose challenges for administrators who wish to set up or maintain inclusive preschool programs.

What Makes Preschool Inclusion Unique?

Inclusion at the preschool level is unique from inclusive programs and practices at the elementary, middle school, and high school levels. Each of the factors identified in the next sections, and undoubtedly others, create a context that differs substantially from inclusion occurring for older children.

* **First**, because public school systems provide programs for typically developing school-age children, the possibility for inclusion exists at the elementary, middle, and high school levels. At the preschool level, however, public school programs are not always provided. Thus, public school inclusion options for preschoolers with disabilities may not be readily available in many school systems.

* **Second**, preschool classrooms differ from typical public school classes for older children on a range of features (e.g., teacher-child ratio, class size, and physical characteristics of the classroom).

* **Third**, the curriculum in early childhood education and early childhood special education differs from the educational curriculum for older children. Early childhood education programs typically follow developmentally appropriate practices that focus on developmental domains and are child-directed. In contrast, curriculum for school-age children is academically oriented and tends to be teacher-directed.

* **Fourth**, the actual developmental skills of young children differ from older children. At a younger age there is less developmental discrepancy between children with disabilities and their same-age peers than occurs in the elementary, middle, and high school grades. Likewise, social relationships with peers are less firmly fixed for young children than for older children.

* **Fifth**, the pressures of high-stakes achievement testing has not been extended down into the preschool years, whereas testing is very evident in elementary school programs and has implications for inclusion at that level.

National Laws and Policies that Underlie Preschool Inclusion

Inclusion for preschool children is pushed by national and state policies. As one administrator told us:

> "We have been instructed by our legal department to carefully look at the least restrictive options for the kids and to justify why we can't provide services in less restrictive settings." -Program Administrator

At the public school level, the *Individuals with Disabilities Education Act* proposes guidelines for early intervention programs operating in different agencies and in preschool programs under the auspices of the public schools. For programs in the community, the *Americans with Disabilities Act* specifies that children cannot be excluded from services, such as in child care centers, private preschools, and other early childhood programs, because of their disability. For *Head Start*, national policy dictates that children with disabilities make up at least 10% of the total number of children receiving services. These laws and national policies create a great impetus for inclusion at the early childhood level, as well as create opportunities for inclusion to occur outside the traditional school setting.

Individuals With Disability Education Act (IDEA)

Federal legislation that prescribes educational policy for students with disabilities began nearly a quarter century ago with PL 94-142. Over the years, provisions were added that expanded the early intervention services to infants and toddlers and ensured that educational services be provided to children 3-5 years old. For both age groups, the law proposes that, to the extent possible, services for infants and toddlers be provided in natural environments, and services for preschool children be located in the least restrictive environment.

Section 612 of IDEA

In general, to the maximum extent appropriate, children with disabilities including children in public or private institutions or other care facilities, are educated with children who are not disabled, and special classes, separate schooling, or other removal of children with disabilities from the regular educational environment occurs only when the nature or severity of the disability of a child is such that education in regular classes with the use of supplementary aids and services cannot be achieved satisfactorily.

Americans With Disability Act (ADA)

Reflecting a societal value that individuals with disabilities should have the same access to activities of daily living as other members of society, Congress passed the Americans with Disability Act in 1990. The implication for preschool inclusion was an opening of doors to child care centers and preschools that previously had not admitted children with disabilities.

ADA

Public Accomodation- The following private entities are considered public accommodations for purposes of this title, if the operations of such entities affect commerce—a NURSERY , elementary, secondary, undergraduate, or postgraduate private school, or other place of education; a DAY CARE CENTER , senior citizen center, homeless shelter, food bank, adoption agency, or other social service center establishment; [emphasis added].

ADA creates the opportunity for families and professionals to find placements for children with disabilities in the same classrooms and programs where typically developing children attend. As we will see in subsequent chapters, however, finding a proper placement is only the first step. Building the professional bridges that ensure quality inclusive programs requires much ongoing effort from everyone involved.

National Head Start Policy

Since the early 1970s, Head Start has been the largest federally funded early childhood program in the country. Head Start provides early childhood education, along with health and family services, to children from low income families. In addition, Head Start has the mandate to enroll children with disabilities.

National Head Start Policy

The Head Start responsibility is to make available directly or in cooperation with other agencies services in the least restrictive environment in accordance with an individualized education program (IEP) for at least TEN PERCENT OF ENROLLED CHILDREN WHO MEET THE DISABILITIES ELIGIBILITY CRITERIA [emphasis added].

For school systems, Head Start's policy could open the door to interagency collaboration. Successful models exist for jointly supporting children in classes that enroll Head Start children and children with disabilities. However, physical placement in the same classroom is just a first step. Professional collaboration is the grease that allows this wheel of inclusion to turn.

Chapter One

Position Statements of National Organizations

In addition to national legislation and policy, inclusion is also supported by professional and parent organizations. Position statements from these organizations are noted.

The Council for Exceptional Children; Division for Early Childhood

The Council for Exceptional Children (CEC) is the largest organization for professionals and others who work with students with disabilities. CEC's Division for Early Childhood (DEC) supports inclusion at the early childhood level.

DEC POLICY

Inclusion, as a value, supports the right of all children, regardless of abilities, to participate actively in natural settings within their communities. Natural settings are those in which the child would spend time had he or she not had a disability. These settings include but are not limited to home, preschool, nursery schools, Head Start programs, kindergartens, neighborhood school classrooms, child care, places of worship, recreational, and other settings that children and families enjoy.

DEC supports and advocates that young children and their families have full and successful access to health, social, educational, and other support services that promote full participation in family and community life. DEC values the cultural, economic, and educational diversity of families and supports a family-guided process for identifying a program of service. As young children participate in group settings (such as preschool, play groups, child care, kindergarten) their active participation should be guided by developmentally and individually appropriate curriculum. Access to and participation in the age appropriate general curriculum becomes central to the identification and provision of specialized support services.

➤

TO IMPLEMENT INCLUSIVE PRACTICES, DEC SUPPORTS

* The continued development, evaluation, and dissemination of full inclusion supports, services, and systems that are of high quality for all children

* The development of preservice and inservice training programs that prepare families, administrators, and service providers to develop and work within inclusive settings

* Collaboration among all key stakeholders to implement flexible fiscal and administrative procedures in support of inclusion

* Research that contributes to our knowledge of recommended practice

* The restructuring and unification of social, educational, health, and intervention supports and services to make them more responsive to the needs of all children and families

---

Adopted 1993; Reaffirmed, 1996; Revised, 2000;
Endorsed by NAEYC - 1994, 1998

National Association for Education of Young Children (NAEYC)

NAEYC is the primary professional organization for educators of young children (birth through 8 years of age). This organization has established guidelines for developmentally appropriate practice for all young children in group or classroom settings. These guidelines set the national standards for acceptable classroom practices in infant and preschool programs.

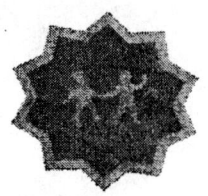

NAEYC PHILOSOPHY ENCOMPASSES A COMMITMENT TO

* Garner the commitment, loyalty, and enthusiasm of thousands of people by providing opportunities for participation, contribution, and building consensus on critical issues

* Value and respect diverse viewpoints and perspectives in all aspects of the practice of early childhood education

* Promote inclusion, access, and nondiscrimination in the full range of programs serving young children, their families, and adults preparing to work in early childhood

* Design programs and services that support individual and collective efforts to improve all early childhood programs that operate with a variety of sponsors, funding sources, and structures

* Encourage and support a strong network of NAEYC affiliates who provide leadership and professional growth opportunities at all levels

* Support the development of individuals' professional competence and attitudes through education, persuasion, and modeling

* Design activities and products that promote recognition of early childhood professional expertise

* Build and maintain a strong organizational structure — governance, communication, financial base, headquarters staff and facility — to provide leadership, coordination, and services

Adopted 1986; Revised 1997

What Is Preschool Inclusion?

The Association for Persons with Severe Disabilities (TASH)

For nearly 30 years, TASH has been a major advocacy organization for persons with disabilities. TASH has supported the inclusion of individuals with disabilities into all aspects of society.

TASH RESOLUTION FOR REGULAR LIVES ISSUES

* Replace institutions with families, homes, community schools and jobs

* Shift away from groupings based on disability to hetero-geneous groupings based on natural diversity

* Education is for all students; not "regular" education and "special" education as separate and unique entities

* Provide the necessary support for students with severe disabilities and for teachers, so that separate schools and separate classrooms can be a thing of the past

* Promote choice-making; learning to exercise responsible control within one's life is part of growing up

* Therapy services need to be integrated into the routines of people's lives while therapists' talents need to be integrated into the educational team

* Children with disabilities need families just as do children who do not have disabilities, and families need support to carry out their critically important job of loving, nourishing, and raising these children with severe disabilities

---

TASH Resolutions, 1989

Chapter One

The Elements of Preschool Inclusion

Certainly, advocacy for inclusion as the primary approach to the education of young children with disabilities is found in both national legislation and policy. Yet, the term "inclusion" provides little information about what makes a program successful. Across the range of studies carried out by investigators with ECRII, we have delineated a set of synthesis points describing elements of inclusion at the preschool level. We conclude this chapter with these points.

ECRII Synthesis Point #1
Inclusion is About Belonging and Participating in a Diverse Society.

* Inclusion is not just a school issue; it extends to the communities in which children and their families live.

* Inclusion is not only a disability issue; all children and families have a right to participate and to be supported in the schools and community.

ECRII Synthesis Point #2
Individuals Define Inclusion Differently.

* Definitions of inclusion are influenced by the varied priorities, responsibilities, and natures of the ecological systems.

* People within the same system (e.g., one school or school district) may have extremely different views of inclusion.

ECRII Synthesis Point #3
Beliefs About Inclusion Influence Its Implementation.

* The beliefs about schooling that families and professionals bring with them to the classroom influence how inclusive practices are planned and implemented; these beliefs are influenced by many complex factors.

* Beliefs about human diversity, that is culture, race, language, class, and ability, influence how inclusion is implemented in schools and communities.

ECRII Synthesis Point #4

Programs, Not Children, Have to be Ready for Inclusion.

* The staff of most of the successful inclusive programs we observed view inclusion as the starting point for all children.

* Inclusion can be appropriate for all children; making it work depends on planning, training, and support.

ECRII Synthesis Point #5

Collaboration is the Cornerstone to Effective Inclusive Programs.

* Collaboration among adults, including professionals and parents, within and across systems and programs, is essential to inclusive programs.

* Collaboration among adults, from different disciplines and often with different philosophies, is one of the greatest challenges to successful implementation of inclusive programs.

> "Our statement of purpose clearly expresses that if we are able to meet a child's needs, regardless of their limitations or special needs, we are going to do it. That has always been our approach."
> -Program Administrator

ECRII Synthesis Point #6

Specialized Instruction is an Important Component of Inclusion.

* Participation in a community based or general education setting is not enough. The individual needs of children with disabilities must be addressed in an inclusive program.

* Specialized instruction can be delivered through a variety of effective strategies, many of which can be embedded in the ongoing classroom activities.

Chapter One

ECRII Synthesis Point #7

Adequate Support is Necessary to Make Inclusive Environments Work.

* Support includes training, personnel, materials, planning time, and ongoing consultation.
* Support can be delivered in different ways, and each person involved in inclusion may have unique needs.

ECRII Synthesis Point #8

Inclusion Can Benefit Children With and Without Disabilities.

* The parents of children without disabilities whose children participate in inclusive programs often report beneficial changes in their children's confidence, self-esteem, and understanding of diversity.
* High quality early childhood programs form the necessary structural base for high quality inclusive programs; thus, all children benefit from them.

"We are not trying to get perfect results. Encourage children to do their work. Give just enough help to move the child on to the next step." -sign posted in art area

Chapter Two

Contexts of Preschool Inclusion

Challenges and Alternatives

If one thinks of preschool inclusion broadly, that is, as young children with disabilities and typically developing children participating together in early childhood programs, there are a lot of ways in which inclusion can occur. For preschool children, inclusion is a way of providing services that fit a child's individual needs, correspond with the wishes of a child's family, and reflect the unique opportunities that exist within a child's community. In the research conducted by ECRII, we found that administrators defined inclusion in substantially different ways. We also learned that inclusive programs fit within different organizational contexts and have different approaches to providing individualized services to children with special needs. Furthermore, within these different organizational contexts, we found both administrative advantages and challenges. In this chapter, we discuss three common organizational contexts in which preschool inclusion exists. We also highlight some of the administrative challenges that accompany each inclusion context and note briefly how some administrators addressed these challenges. In the later chapters of this guide, we provide more detailed alternatives to these challenges.

Organizational Contexts

Organizational context refers to the administrative agency or agencies through which inclusive services are provided. If children with disabilities have IEPs, then one organizational context is the public school system. Examples of inclusive preschool programs within the public school system are programs for young children at-risk for school problems (i.e., Title 1 classes), Public School Head Start programs, and tuition-based programs. As we discussed earlier, however, all public school systems do not provide preschool classes

for typically developing children, thus two other organizational contexts, Head Start and community-based private child care are options for pre-school inclusion. In Table 1, we provide examples of organizational contexts for each of these inclusion options.

Advantages, Challenges, and Alternatives Within the Organizational Contexts

Although there are administrative advantages to each organizational context into which preschool inclusive services are provided, there are administrative challenges as well. We found, however, that administrators who wanted to create and maintain high quality inclusive options for young children with disabilities were very creative in their approaches to solving some of these administrative challenges. We next discuss the advantages of providing preschool inclusive options in the three organizational contexts. We also describe administrative challenges presented by the different organizational contexts and share some alternatives for meeting and solving those challenges.

Advantages to the Public School Organizational Context

When early childhood classes are based in the public schools, logistical problems such as paying child-care tuition, providing transportation, and dealing with different regulations are typically avoided. Another advantage is that teachers are employed by the school system. In many systems, teachers are required to have certification and training exceeding that found in community-based programs. Furthermore, school administrators have more control over the quality of public school-based early childhood classroom than classrooms in community-based or Head Start programs (i.e., number of children, teacher to child ratio, curriculum, materials, and equipment).

ORGANIZATIONAL CONTEXTS FOR PRESCHOOL INCLUSION

Public School Programs as a Context for Inclusion

- Public school preschool programs for children who are educationally at-risk because of family or other circumstances (sometimes Title I funds support these programs)

- Public school Head Start programs

- Special education classes converted to include children without disabilities

- Tuition-based classes in which parents of typically developing children pay fees for their child to attend a public school child care program

Community-Based Child Care as a Context for Inclusion

- Corporate, for-profit national programs like *Kindercare*

- Locally owned programs operated by individuals or community organizations

- Mother's Day Out programs at a local church or community center

- Nonprofit preschools for children from low-income families

Head Start as a Context for Inclusion

- Local Head Start programs operated by community agencies and typically housed in a local community or school district facility

- Regional Head Start program operated by an agency other than the public school system and serving children in classrooms stretching across many communities

Table 1 from Odom, et al., 1999

Flexibility may also be an administrative advantage to early childhood programs in the public schools. A variety of organizational options may be available to the creative administrator. For example, a public school-based inclusive child care program that participated in our research was located in a local high school. The teacher was certified and trained in special education, and high school students served as assistant teachers. In another program, a special education teacher was the lead teacher in a class consisting primarily of children with disabilities, but three or four typically developing children were included as peer models. Although "reverse mainstreaming" programs may not meet some professionals' definition of inclusion, it was a means of offering inclusion in that particular school system.

> a public school-based inclusive child care program that participated in our research was located in a local high school; high school students served as assistant teachers.

Challenges of the Public School Organizational Context

A major challenge of the public school organizational context is administrative structure. Often, the special education program is in one administrative unit and the early childhood education program is in another unit. When this occurs, communication break-downs between the units can be common. For example, we worked with a large urban school system that did not have a preschool program for typically developing children, but provided educational services for preschool children with disabilities in community-based programs. When administrators from another unit within the school system established preschool classes for children at-risk for school problems, they did not consider making some placements available for children with disabilities. In fact, when this plan was presented as a possibility, the administrators expressed resistance.

Another challenge presented by the public school organizational context is finding acceptable inclusive placements. When a school system does

not provide preschool programs for typically developing children, Head Start (administered by the school system) and state-funded preschools for at-risk children may seem a likely inclusion alternative. Some parents and teachers, however, may not view these classrooms as appropriate inclusive options, thereby presenting an administrative challenge.

Another potential challenge of the public school organizational context occurs when there are fee-for-service or tuition-based programs. This type of arrangement may present challenges in both funding and public perception. In many public school systems, the financial structure is not equipped to receive payment from parents for their typically developing children's participation in programs. In fact, in some systems there may be regulations against such payments being made to schools. In addition, public school child care programs are sometimes perceived by the early childhood community as being in competition with private child care. We found there was a perception of unfairness because school-based child care programs were supplemented by the public school system. We also found that the tuition-based public school programs sometimes led to an inadvertent segregation by income level. Parents of typically developing children who pay tuition are more likely to be of higher income families who can afford the tuition. Most children in Head Start and state-funded preschools for children at-risk, however, are more likely to come from lower income families. Middle-income parents of a child with disabilities, then, were likely to select the tuition-based programs for their child because of the class makeup. In our study, the school system permitted this choice as long as parents provided transportation. A final administrative challenge of the public school organizational context is space. In some systems, finding even minimally adequate classroom space presents a significant challenge.

> In some systems, finding even minimally adequate classroom space presents a significant challenge.

Chapter Two

Alternatives to the Challenges of the Public School Organizational Context

Many administrators are very creative when it comes to meeting challenges. For example, in a public school program operated with different administrative units, one key administrator reorganized the administrative structure so that all programs for young children (with or without disabilities) were in one administrative unit. This placed the supervisors of the early childhood education and early childhood special education programs in the same office area rather than in different parts of the city. Furthermore, the reorganization allowed the creation of a more proactive policy related to inclusion and early childhood services.

"Because I carefully document all the services children receive, I don't feel compelled to establish different classes just because funding streams are different." - School System Administrator

Another creative administrator found an alternative to the challenge of income segregation by establishing classes for children funded by different programs. In this arrangement, children from Head Start, state-funded preschool programs, and tuition-based programs were brought together into generic early childhood classrooms, which also served as inclusive classrooms. Blended classrooms such as this could be located in an early childhood center where services to many children are provided or located in a public school building within the local community. Administratively, a blended arrangement facilitates (and in fact requires) flexibility in how children are placed in classrooms. Mixing children with different funding streams requires a creative blending of funds from different sources, however, it can be done.

Advantages of the Community-based Child Care Organizational Context

Often, the primary advantage to inclusive community-based programs is location. Sometimes the program is close to a family's home and perhaps siblings attend the center. In requesting placement in a community-based center, one parent of a child with autism told us:

> "We feel it is important for Jimmy to be in the same center with his sister, because it is a good place for him to learn. He needs to be around kids who can serve as role models. Basically he needs to see it; he needs to be around it as much as he can." - Parent

By being located close to the child's home, Jimmy could be included more actively in the community. In some ways, this is similar to elementary-school children attending their neighborhood school rather than being bused outside the community.

Challenges of the Community-based Child Care Organizational Context

Many challenges exist for creating and maintaining inclusive options for children with disabilities in community-based child care centers. A primary challenge is funding—who pays tuition? In some states, laws or policies prevent local program administrators from spending special education dollars to pay private preschool tuition. Other challenges are finding suitable, high-quality centers and establishing a working relationship with child care providers when inclusive options are being established. Although parents should be given a voice in the selection of a child care center, balancing the perspectives of parents and educators can be a challenge. For example, the parent may believe a selected center is appropriate and desirable for their child and the school district may perceive the program as being of poor quality and undesirable. Another challenge of the community-based context is employee status. Teachers in many

Although parents should be given a voice in the selection of a child care, balancing the perspectives of parents and educators can be a challenge.

community-based programs are typically not employed by the school system, thus it may be difficult for the school system to establish individualized programs for children with disabilities which the staff in the center should carry out. Finally, a big challenge of the community-based context is transportation. With child care centers located in various parts of a city, arranging transportation may be complex. Also, local policies may prevent the school from providing transportation to the private center, so the transportation task may fall to the parents.

Alternatives to the Challenges of Community-based Child Care Organizational Context

If early childhood programs for typically developing children are not operating in a public school system, we found that school systems were likely to provide inclusion options within community-based preschool programs. Typically, itinerant teachers and assistant teachers were employed by the public school system in an effort to provide special education services. The issue of child care tuition, however, was a sticking point for many programs. Some programs addressed the issue by paying tuition for an "educationally relevant" portion of the day (i.e., a 3- or 4-hour period). If parents wanted their child in the program for the remainder of the day, they paid the additional tuition. Although this option provided some parents with an active choice about the type of educational program their child received, the educationally relevant alternative is not possible in states where policy and regulations prohibit any payment of child care tuition. For parents who cannot afford to pay tuition to a community-based program, such restrictive tuition policies limit their options. In some states, however, administrators found public funds to pay tuition or defray expenses for families who could not afford the child care tuition. Administrators need to be on the lookout for creative options to the funding challenges. With the recent changes in welfare funding and national interest in providing preschool education for all children, funding alternatives are becoming more available.

Locating and establishing a working relationship with child care programs presents another major challenge. If an administrator or school system makes the decision to use community-based programs, he/she must undergo a search for appropriate centers. School systems must, therefore, get the word out to community-based programs. In larger communities with formal or informal child care networks, information can be passed to directors or coordinators of early childhood programs. Corporate child care organizations routinely meet with their center directors, so forwarding information through the local corporate office is an option. In small communities with few child care centers, hosting a meeting for child care directors at the public school office (be sure to have food and drink) or talking individually with directors are two productive approaches.

An important part of establishing a working relationship between organizations is making expectations clear. Negotiating and specifying, in advance, the responsibilities of both center-based child care personnel and public school personnel is necessary. One system with which we worked designed a formal contract that specified the tuition to be paid, hours children would attend, and responsibilities of the staff members. Another alternative is to establish an interagency agreement that is specific, but less prescriptive in nature.

The issue of child care quality also is important. The foundation for providing high quality inclusive programs, is having high quality *early childhood* programs. Only child care centers with high quality programs should be invited into a partnership. When using this approach, however, political fallout within the community can occur, especially if someone thinks that their program is considered low quality. A possible route around this problem is to work through parents by providing information about the important characteristics of a high quality early childhood program (see chapter 3). Then, a school system representative and the parents could visit programs together, giving the parents an opportunity to make an informed choice about their child's program. From our research, it appeared that a sustained and positive working relationship developed naturally when the school system established the community-based partnership in high quality programs. Both school system and parents saw the program doing an effective job of providing learning opportunities for children with disabilities as well as for children without disabilities.

Another community-based option is for the school system to routinely purchase slots for children with disabilities in high quality programs where it is expected parents might want to send their children. In some systems, however, the issue of quality in community-based programs has not been a concern that could be addressed satisfactorily. In our study, a large metropolitan system decided to provide inclusive opportunities for children in early childhood programs operating within their system (i.e., the public school alternative mentioned previously). This reduced the opportunity for and the emphasis on community-based child care programs.

Establishing individualized educational services for children with disabilities in community-based settings also presents a challenge. Training for early childhood staff is extremely important. Such training should address both the attitudinal aspects of providing inclusive services for children with disabilities and specific teaching approaches. (More information about training and personnel development appears in chapter 5.) Having the early childhood teacher participate in IEP conferences also is very important. In the IEP conference, early childhood educators learn about a child's goals and objectives and have opportunities to contribute to the development of the IEP. If the IEP meeting cannot be held at a convenient time for the early childhood teacher, coverage should be provided (e.g., a temporary substitute). In many community-based programs, an itinerant teacher is assigned to work with the child with disabilities. Itinerant teachers also need to spend time with a child's teacher to work on establishing learning opportunities that specifically address the child's goals and objectives. (More information about collaboration appears in Chapter 4.)

The development and use of activities that create learning opportunities require a great deal of collaboration between itinerant service providers and early childhood staff. Programs in which administrators support the development of collaborative relationships (e.g., by providing time for joint planning and communication) provide more positive inclusive experiences for children than do programs in which this administrative support is absent. Sometimes public school systems provide an assistant teacher to work directly in the inclusive classroom. (Hopefully this assistant teacher is someone with training or experience with children with disabilities!) The role of the assistant teacher may vary, but in successful programs, the assistant sometimes works directly with the child with disabilities and at other times with other children in the classroom allowing time for the early childhood teacher to work with the child with disabilities.

Transportation is yet another major issue for school systems. A sizable portion of a school system budget is allocated to transportation, and the logistics of providing transportation are sometime overwhelming. National public policy dictates that transportation is provided for children with disabilities. School systems have addressed the complicated task of providing transportation to local child care centers in several ways. For some children, school systems provide the standard school bus mode of transportation. If a number of children and child care centers are located in the same community, it may be feasible for a school van to take children from their homes directly to the center. In the ECRII study, one program contracted with a private transportation service operating in their city, however, this is highly idiosyncratic and may not work well in other locations. In other programs, the school system paid parents to transport their children, although state policies prohibited another program from using special education funds to pay parents for providing transportation. Sometimes, parents may choose to transport their child to a particular inclusive program despite the personal cost.

Chapter Two

Advantages of the Head Start Organizational Context

National Head Start policy dictates that at least 10% of the children receiving Head Start services be children with disabilities, and in recent years, the push has been toward providing services to children with substantial disabilities. This national policy has affected the interest and intent of Head Start directors to include children with disabilities in their centers. Although Head Start has income guidelines that families must meet in order for their children to qualify, income waivers may sometimes be available for children with disabilities. Such policies may create opportunities for public school systems to establish inclusive options for children with disabilities in local Head Start programs that are operated by community agencies.

In the ECRII research, we found that classrooms in Head Start programs often provided high-quality early childhood education and had resources such as materials and space that did not exist in some community-based programs. Furthermore, Head Start staff routinely received training on a variety of early childhood issues, and the programs often followed a standard curriculum. In many Head Start centers, services to families (i.e., assistance from a family services coordinator, parent groups, etc.) and health services for children were available. We also found an element of belonging for all children that we saw as a positive characteristic of inclusion. A Head Start administrator expressed to us:

> "Our preschool and Head Start are very much a part of our school family. They are included on our teams even though they technically are just housed in the building. We try hard to make them feel a part . . . and in terms of Kenny [a child with disabilities] we all see it as our role to make him fit in — to just be a part of the group."

Challenges to the Head Start Organizational Context

In using Head Start as an inclusive option for children with disabilities, several administrative challenges exist. In some programs, we found minimal contact between school system staff and the Head Start program staff. IEPs were developed through the school district, related services were sometimes provided by the school district (e.g., speech pathology, occupational therapy), and sometimes transportation was provided by the school district. The early childhood teachers from the Head Start program, however, did not have an opportunity to meet, consult, or collaborate with the special education staff in the school district (or even see the IEP). Although children with disabilities may have received a high-quality early childhood program, individual programs to meet their specific goals and objectives were not planned or used. Providing an individualized program in some Head Start classes is a challenge.

philosophical differences between special education personnel and Head Start teachers created a challenge to inclusive Head Start classrooms

Another challenge, is forming collaborative relationships between school system personnel and Head Start staff. Head Start centers often adopt an established curriculum and are supervised to determine how well they follow the curriculum. Typically, these curricula follow a developmental appropriate practice orientation and when strictly implemented, leave little room for individualized or small-group teaching strategies sometime used by special education personnel. Thus, we found that philosophical differences (related to the curriculum) between special education personnel and Head Start teachers created a substantial challenge in some inclusive Head Start classrooms.

Different schedules and administrative guidelines in Head Start programs and public school programs also present a challenge. Because school boards determine the calendar for the school system, and Head Start agencies determine their schedules, Head Start classes may begin and end on different dates. Consequently, teaching staff and children with special needs sometimes begin school weeks before Head Start children and staff. Such a mismatch may lead to difficulties in joint planning and class scheduling.

Chapter Two

Other issues arise when guidelines for certain features of the programs, like transportation, differ across systems. For example, we observed organizational regulations that resulted in public schools providing transportation for children with disabilities and Head Start providing transportation for Head Start children. Children in these programs lived in the same community yet the policy restrictions resulted in children riding separate buses and even arriving and departing at different times. These policies also created complications around who could ride what bus on field trips.

Last, because Head Start is designed for children from low-income families there is a perception that it is not a good inclusion option because it is not a typcial program. The assumption is that children in Head Start need extra developmental and health services in order to be prepared for elementary school and later life and they are thus an at-risk population. In some communities, the dialect or actual language spoken may differ from the mainstream community. We found that some parents and administrators who held this perception voiced concerns about children with disabilities being placed in such environments (Please note that this is not our view, in fact, we generally found Head Start classrooms to be good places for all children).

Alternatives to the Challenges of the Head Start Organizational Context

The obvious solution to lack of contact between Head Start and public school personnel is to increase contact. In the programs we observed, this happened in two ways. Some public school systems provided itinerant teachers and assistant teachers for children with disabilities in Head Start. However, as with the community-based context, this solution was effective only when school system teachers collaborated with Head Start teachers in an effort to provide quality individualized services for the children with disabilities.

The second approach was to form co-teaching classes. In these classes a Head Start teacher and a public school special education teacher shared

Some children in these programs lived in the same community yet the policy restrictions resulted in children riding separate buses and even arriving and departing at different times.

the lead-teacher role. In addition, sometimes assistant teachers were funded by each organization. Teachers collaborated to plan and run activities in the classroom. We found that in co-teaching classes, more children with special needs were often enrolled than in community-based programs. In order to be successful, however, it is important that both teachers plan the class before the start of the school year. Allocated planning time for teachers also is important. In successful programs, public school staff and Head Start staff share the responsibilities for all the children, with the special education teacher taking the lead in planning or modifying individual activities for children with disabilities. Support from both Head Start and public school administrators for teachers to assume this less traditional co-teaching role and provide time to accomplish the needed planning is an essential influence on the effect of the program. We discuss co-teaching arrangements in more detail in Chapter 4.

Philosophical differences do emerge, and some program directors and teachers have been successful in dealing with them. An important way to address these differences is to openly discuss program and curriculum philosophy before the program begins (or at least at the beginning of the school year). Understanding each perspective that exists in the classroom is very important, and building respect for different philosophies is essential. Flexibility and reasonable compromise is essential for making co-teaching programs run well. For example, in the field of special education, there has been a substantial movement toward the use of naturalistic teaching approaches. These approaches typically fit well with most early childhood curricula and are effective for many children. Adopting a naturalistic teaching approach rather than a more structured, didactic approach, could make the instruction for children with special needs more compatible with the early childhood curriculum. On the other hand, it would be important for the Head Start administrators and teachers to allow some flexibility in the way the early childhood curriculum is implemented in order to address the needs of children with disabilities. For some children, an individual or small group, a direct instructional format may be the best way to introduce new skills. Planning ways to fit such instruction into the class schedule is very important. One Head Start administrator described

Chapter Two

her philosophy of including children with disabilities in this way:

> "We try to treat the children with special needs just like the other children. After all they are ALL children. Here everyone is a 'Head Start kid,' we just don't consider them 'special-ed kids'."

Administrators can assist greatly in addressing the issues of scheduling and regulations. Taking a problem-solving attitude, rather than a traditional this-is-how-we-do-it approach is essential. In one successful Head Start-public school inclusive program, administrators arranged to have the same start date at the beginning of school year for both programs. Likewise, administrators and teachers from both programs reviewed school calendars and identified compatible holidays. Although this did not work perfectly, and there were some days when only one group attended, (i.e., the public schools had more days in their school year than Head Start), minimizing incompatibilities in the schedule was a key problem administrators could solve. Furthermore, as an alternative to some of the transportation challenges, organizations established shared services. This option allowed all children to ride the same bus, regardless of which organization officially provided the financial support.

Summary

The contexts for providing inclusive preschool services for children with disabilities differ from system to system. Although we categorized the organizational structures into three general contexts, most school systems create inclusive options for preschool children that fit the unique organizational context of their system. Nevertheless, challenges exist for all organizational contexts and creative administrators find alternatives to overcome them. In the remainder of this guide, we provide information that can help you create high quality inclusive preschool programs as a viable option for children with disabilities and their families.

Taking a problem-solving attitude, rather than a traditional this-is-how-we-do-it approach is essential

ECRII Administrators' Guide

Chapter Three

Quality of Inclusion

Quality of Inclusion: Jumping the Hurdles

When parents and professionals are asked to state their concerns about preschool inclusion, quality of the early childhood program is often mentioned. As applied to preschool inclusion, quality may refer to either the general early childhood environment for all children, or it may be defined more narrowly as quality of inclusion for children with disabilities within the early childhood setting. Thus, we have come to think of these two quality dimensions as hurdles, both of which must be jumped if preschool inclusion is to work well. Furthermore, we believe these hurdles must be jumped in order, that is physically placing children within disabilities into a high-quality early childhood settings (or jumping only the first hurdle) does not ensure high quality inclusion services will occur. In fact, a major finding of our research institute, ECRII synthesis points 6, states: Specialized instruction is an important component of inclusion.

Significant administrative support is necessary to clear both of these quality hurdles successfully. In this chapter, we discuss ways in which administrators can support their programs in providing both high-quality early childhood and high-quality early childhood inclusion. Specifically, we address the following:

- Quality in the regular early childhood program

- High quality early childhood programs as a necessary, but not sufficient, environment for inclusion

- Quality of individualized services within high quality inclusive preschool programs

- Tools for building and maintaining high-quality inclusive preschool programs

Chapter Three

Characteristics of Quality in the Early Childhood Setting

More than a decade ago, the National Association for the Education of Young Children (NAEYC) published a position statement that emphasized three core beliefs:

- **Children have a right to attend good programs that promote their development and learning**

- **Child care centers should ensure their staff are well-prepared, competent, and adequately compensated**

- **Families should have access to affordable, high-quality child care [emphasis added].**

When defining and evaluating quality in child care, two dimensions are typically considered. First is the quality of regulatable items. These items which typically are defined by numbers include: adult-to-child ratio, group size, caregiver education, caregiver salaries, and staff turnover. The second quality dimension relates to the *environmental* features of the program such as adult-child interactions and curriculum.

Over the years, several instruments for rating and evaluating both the regulatable quality and environmental quality have been developed. Two commonly used measures are the *Early Childhood Environment Rating Scale—Revised* (ECERS-R; Harms, Clifford, & Cryer, 1998), and *The Classroom Practice Inventory* (CPI; Hyson, Hirsh-Pasek, & Rescorla, 1990). Both of these measures are consistent with the NAEYC Developmentally Appropriate Practices (DAP) guidelines described by Bredekamp and Copple (1997). Although the ECERS-R and the CPI do not address the special learning needs of young children with disabilities, they provide clear guidelines for general early childhood education program quality.

 Quality of Inclusion

Because successful inclusion can exist only in high quality preschool programs, we recommend evaluating the quality of any preschool being considered as an inclusion site. Table 1 shows a summarized version of the CPI, which may be used as an initial evaluation of possible inclusion sites. Parents making decisions about programs for their child with disabilities also might find Table 1 useful.

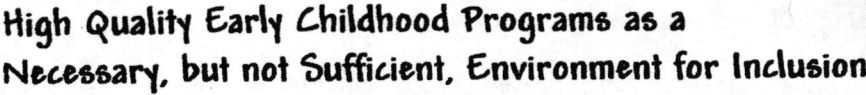

High Quality Early Childhood Programs as a Necessary, but not Sufficient, Environment for Inclusion

A high quality early childhood program is a necessary foundation of preschool inclusion. To be sufficient, however, the program must ensure that developmental needs of young children with disabilities are met. Thus, when a child with disability is placed in an inclusive program, the bar is raised on the quality dimension. Specifically, this means the quality of inclusion also must be considered.

High-quality inclusion means that opportunities for a child to meet the goals and objectives stated on the Individualized Educational Program (IEP) occur during the ongoing routines and activities of the high quality preschool program. Individualizing a child's program, however, requires considerable effort and support. Children with disabilities must have the same opportunities to participate as typically developing children and their preschool teachers and assistants also must know how to embed the individualized programs into the ongoing activities and routines.

We noted earlier that many measures of classroom quality do not consider the needs of children with disabilities. Our colleagues Carl Dunst and Melinda Raab, however, have developed the *Preschool Assessment of the Classroom Environment-Revised (PACE-R)*, a classroom quality measure for inclusive preschool programs. In Table 2 we summarize the assessment items on the *PACE-R*. We encourage you to become familiar with these areas of inclusion quality.

Chapter Three

QUALITY INDICATORS FOR ALL PRESCHOOL PROGRAMS

Program and Activity Focus

- *Children* select activities from a variety of learning areas, including dramatic play, blocks, science, math, games and puzzles, books, art, and music

- *Children* are involved in concrete, three-dimensional learning activities, with materials closely related to their daily life experiences

- *Children* are physically active in the classroom, spontaneously initiating many of their own activities and choosing from activities the teacher has prepared

- *Children* work individually or in small, child-chosen groups; different children are doing different things

- *Children* use a variety of art media, such as easel painting, finger painting, and clay modeling, in ways of their choosing

- *Children* have daily opportunities to listen to and read stories, dictate stories, notice print being used, engage in dramatic play, and experiment with writing by drawing, copying, and inventing their own spelling

- *Children* have daily opportunities to use pegboards, puzzles, Legos, markers, scissors, and other similar materials in ways of their choosing

- *Teachers* ask questions that encourage children to give more than one right answer

- *Teachers* use activities such as block building, cooking, and woodworking to help children learn concepts in math, science, and social studies

- *Teachers* involve children in activities by stimulating their natural curiosity and interests

Emotional Climate

- *Teachers* show affection by smiling, touching, holding, and speaking to children at their eye level throughout the day, but especially at arrival and departure times

- *Teachers* use redirection, positive reinforcement, and encouragement as guidance or as discipline techniques

- *Environment* is characterized by pleasant conversation, spontaneous laughter, and exclamations of excitement

---

Table 1

Adapted from the Classroom Practice Inventory; Hyson, Hirsh-Pasek, & Rescorla, 1990).

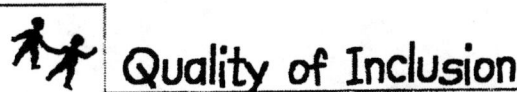

Quality of Individualized Services Within a High Quality Inclusive Program

High quality individualized services are specific and intense, and they ensure young children with disabilities make progress. Administrators can support high quality individualized service provision in many ways. Before we discuss these support mechanisms, however, we need to clarify an often misunderstood term. *Individualized* DOES NOT mean that teachers always must provide a one-to-one program of instruction, although this sometimes may happen for some children. *Individualized* DOES mean that teachers ensure young children with disabilities make progress on their individualized goals by embedding regular and frequent learning opportunities into the ongoing routines and activities of the classroom.

> "I think that is one reason why preschool special ed mainstreaming or full inclusion works out so well is because many of our children have similar goals. There are usually other children at the same level, doing some of the same activities." -Early Childhood Teacher

The Individualized Educational Program

Administrators should ensure that every child's IEP is developed by a team that consists of not only educators and specialists, but also a representative from the child's family. The family should have opportunity to share the goals they have for their child and together the team should determine what goals are reasonable to target for the IEP. Goals should be functional, that is they should teach behaviors or skills that are immediately useful or lead to skills that will be useful in children's lives. For example, teaching a child the names of preferred toys is much more functional than teaching him or her to say the names of zoo animals presented on picture cards. Knowing toy names facilitates language and communication about the child's immediate world. The immediate benefit of naming zoo animals is not so obvious.

ECRII Administrators' Guide

Chapter Three

QUALITY INDICATORS FOR INCLUSIVE PRESCHOOL PROGRAMS

Program Foundation and Philosophy

· High quality programs are guided by a clearly described philosophy, have written goals and objectives, and promote partnerships with parents.

Management and Training

· In high quality programs, the director communicates expectations to staff, regularly visits classrooms and monitors staff performance, provides ongoing support and feedback, and arranges for on-the-job-training.

Environmental Organization

· High quality programs have open classrooms clearly divided into learning areas with appropriate, child-sized equipment and furniture. Material selection is adequate, accessible, and developmentally appropriate.

Staffing Patterns

· In high quality programs, staff schedules and responsibilities are defined and followed; staff prepare activities in advance, and staff has time to plan and exchange information.

Instructional Content

· In high quality programs, functional skills are targeted for instruction, and instruction takes place during naturally occurring classroom routines. Learning activities are developmentally appropriate, and multiple activity options are scheduled and available to children throughout the day. Children do not wait for activities to begin or end.

Instructional Techniques

· In high quality programs, staff responds to child-initiated behaviors, uses appropriate strategies to facilitate practice and learning, and provides individualized attention during activities. Behavior management procedures are planned and used consistently.

Program Evaluation

· In high quality programs, the program has a written plan to monitor goals and objectives. Evaluation is conducted regularly and data used to make decisions toward improvement.

Table 2 from Preschool Assessment of Classroom Environment Scale-Revised; Raab & Dunst,1997.

Implementing the Individualized Educational Program

Predictable routines and activities are essential components of high quality early childhood programs and are especially important for effective and efficient implementation of a young child's IEP. A good classroom schedule, however, involves more than just stating the times when specific activities will occur. To learn how IEPs are implemented, our research institute conducted focus groups across the country with early childhood teachers, teaching assistants, administrators, and special service providers. Based on the information we gathered from these service providers, we developed a teacher resource guide, *Building Blocks for Successful Early Childhood Programs* (Sandall et al., 2000); hereafter called *Building Blocks*. Listed below are seven characteristics of a good classroom schedule from *Building Blocks*.

- Day is divided into time segments that are appropriate to children's needs and abilities

- Schedule offers a balance of active and quiet times

- Schedule provides times for large and small group activities, and times to play alone or with others

- Outdoor time is scheduled

- Schedule offers a balance of child-initiated activities and teacher-directed activities

- Schedule includes adequate time for routines (such as toileting and snacks) and transitions

- Schedule maximizes teaching and learning time

Scheduled activities, however, do not guarantee a child will make progress on individual learning objectives. To ensure that children with disabilities make progress, teaching plans must provide children with many learning opportunities. Teachers must evaluate the scheduled routines and activi-

Chapter Three

ties and determine when opportunities exist for children with disabilities to practice skills identified in their objectives. Whenever possible, instruction should be embedded into the schedule. Listed below are some examples of embedding learning opportunities. For a detailed discussion of this procedure, we refer you to *Building Blocks*.

- Teaching the child to say "more" during block play
- Teaching the names of clothing items during dress-up or dramatic play
- Teaching the names of foods during snack and meal time
- Teaching grasping during puzzles (e. g., picking up a puzzle piece)
- Teaching grasping during art (e. g., picking up pieces of tape)
- Teaching shoe tying after nap

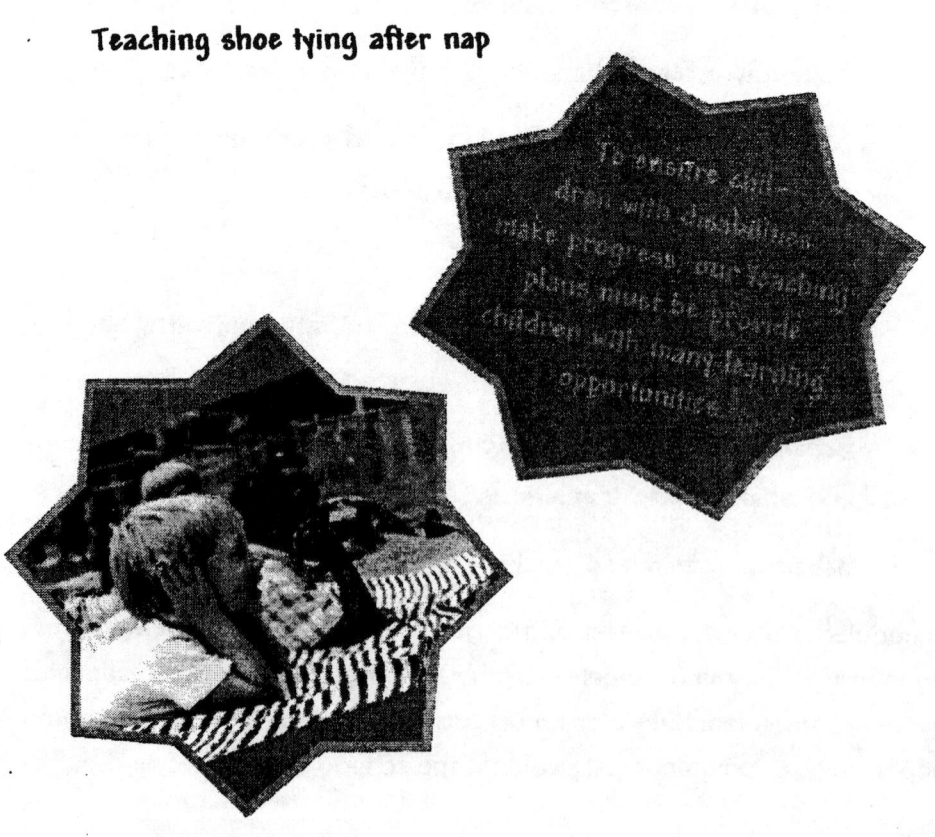

To ensure children with disabilities make progress, our teaching plans must be provide children with many learning opportunities.

A basic planning tool for facilitating instruction around a child's IEP is the goal-by-activity matrix (see example below). A goal-by-activity matrix is a simple grid that allows a teacher to plan when, throughout a child's day, important goals are addressed, and who is responsible for implementing the procedure. Typically, individual events or routines are listed down the left column of the matrix, and either individual children or specific goals are listed across the top row of the matrix. Teaching and learning opportunities are then identified and marked in the appropriate boxes. In our example, the matrix is designed to indicate when during the day the teacher (Mrs. Taylor) will implement specific instructional plans for three students (Tina, Terrance, and Kim).

Mrs. Taylor	Tina	Terrance	Kim
Arrival	Transition	Identify name	Picture schedule
Planning	Request & comment		
Centers	Sharing	Play near peers	Picture schedule & timer
Recall	Use words	Use descriptive words	
Snack	Requests		
Outdoor		Play near peers	
Small Group	Request & share	Use descriptive words	
Large Group	Requests	Identify name	
Departure	Fastening		

Chapter Three

Another important consideration related to providing high-quality inclusive services is how and when to use specialized instructional strategies. Early childhood staff need information about strategies available for specialized instruction, and they need to know when and how to use the strategies. Early intervention strategies can range from something as simple as stabilizing a toy with Velcro or non-skid backing to a very sophisticated prompting strategy that teaches a child to grasp an object or request a drink. From the focus group research, we identified eight categories of teacher-friendly curriculum and material modifications (listed in Table 3). Many of these easy-to-implement curriculum modification strategies require the staff only to plan ahead what and how they provide learning opportunities for children with disabilities. Specialized instructional strategies, however, require staff training and practice. For detailed information about specialized strategies we again refer you to the *Building Blocks*.

Staff Monitoring and Evaluation

The final component of high-quality inclusive preschool programs is staff monitoring and evaluation. On-going monitoring in the domain is a phrase often associated with school-age special education, but it applies to early childhood special education as well. Monitoring child performance on targeted goals should be ongoing. Staff should develop formal data collection procedures so monitoring is systematic and useful. Many times a simple check-sheet is all that is needed. Monitoring is the *means* not the *end*. A child's performance data should be evaluated regularly and used to guide program revisions and changes.

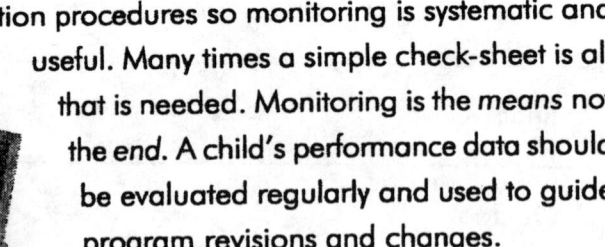

BUILDING BLOCKS CURRICULUM MODIFICATIONS AND ADAPTATIONS

Environmental Support
- Adapt the physical, social, and temporal environment to promote participation, engagement, and learning

Materials Adaptation
- Modify materials so that the child can participate as independently as possible

Simplify the Activity
- Simplify a complicated task by breaking it into smaller parts or reducing the number of steps

Child Preference
- Use a favorite toy, activity, or person to encourage child participation in learning activities

Special Equipment
- Use special or adaptive devices to increase a child's level of participation

Adult Support
- Use adult intervention such as modeling, joining child in play, praising, and giving encouragement to support the child's participation

Peer Support
- Utilize peers as models and helpers, or to provide praise and encouragement

Invisible Support
- Ensure that naturally occurring events (e.g. child's turn, opportunity to use materials) are purposefully arranged so the child has a learning opportunity

Table 3
from *Building Blocks for Successful Early Childhood Programs*; Sandall, et al., 2000

Tools for Building and Maintaining High-Quality Inclusive Preschool Programs

In earlier sections of this chapter, we provided some assessment tools to facilitate your efforts at developing high-quality inclusion programs. Those tools should provide you with important information about the environmental quality of your inclusive program. Identifying areas of strengths and needs related to the quality of inclusive services also must be considered. We end this chapter by providing a check-sheet for evaluating inclusive quality. The check-sheet is based on several resources, specifically the *Quality Indicators: Early Childhood Special Education*, (University of Washington, 1996); the *PACE-R* (Raab & Dunst, 1997); the *Quality of Inclusive Experiences Measure* (Wolery, Paucca, Brashers, & Grant, 1999); Jones and Rapport (1997), and work from the ECRII. This check-sheet should provide you with initial information for building or maintaining a quality inclusion program. For a more in-depth and formal evaluation of your program, we recommend the abbreviated or the comprehensive version of the *Quality of Inclusive Experiences Measure* (Wolery et al., 1999).

EVALUATING QUALITY IN THE INCLUSIVE PRESCHOOL PROGRAM

<u>Program Philosophy that Supports Inclusion</u>

_____ Philosophy states the program's goals, objectives, and definition of inclusion
_____ Philosophy indicates program's commitment to parents
_____ Philosophy is supported by all staff

<u>Adequate Space, Equipment, and Materials</u>

_____ Classroom areas accessible to all children
_____ Children with physical disabilities able to move about classroom with least restrictive form of mobility
_____ Room arrangement flexible so changes and adaptations are easy
_____ Room arrangement accommodates close proximity to peers
_____ Functional signs and picture schedules facilitate transitions
_____ Variety of developmentally appropriate materials are available
_____ Equipment and material adaptations are made as needed
_____ Outdoor equipment facilitates opportunities for children with disabilities to engage with their peers in outdoor play

<u>Staff Management and Training</u>

_____ Staff is knowledgeable of child development and instructional strategies
_____ Staff has written job descriptions to define their roles
_____ Staff has ongoing training and support to implement therapy interventions and to use adapted equipment
_____ Staff knows where, what, and with whom they should be working
_____ Staff has regular meeting times and opportunities for staff development
_____ Staff feels supported by administration

<u>Individualizing the Curriculum and Instruction</u>

_____ Goals for children with disabilities are functional, and instruction is embedded into ongoing routines and activities
_____ Communication goals for children with disabilities facilitate child-child interactions and adult-child interactions

Chapter Three

_____ Therapy goals are implemented throughout the day

_____ Children have multiple times throughout the day to practice and learn individualized goals

_____ Children with disabilities are taught specific play skills to facilitate engagement with materials and peers

_____ Children with disabilities participate in the same activities, routines, and transitions as other children in the class

_____ Curriculum and materials are modified as needed so children with disabilities can participate as independently as possible

_____ Planned cues and prompts for children with challenging behaviors are used consistently

Staff Planning and Implementation

_____ Staff plans a daily schedule that includes predictable routines and activities

_____ Staff facilitates child engagement and play using naturalistic techniques when possible and systematic prompts when needed

_____ Staff provides opportunities for children to make choices, negotiate conflicts, and problem solve

_____ Staff physically locates themselves so children orient toward other children

_____ Staff adapts environment to promote participation, engagement, and learning

_____ Staff modifies materials or equipment so children with disabilities can participate as independently as possible

_____ Staff simplifies complicated tasks by breaking them into smaller parts or reducing number of steps

_____ Staff utilizes child preference to increase engagement

_____ Staff engages in play with children to model use of materials and play themes, and to facilitate communication and social interactions

Staff Monitoring and Evaluation

_____ Ongoing monitoring of child performance on targeted goals is maintained; data used to evaluate and revise intervention programs

_____ Child engagement in routines and activities is continually monitored, and environmental changes are made when indicated

Table 4 adapted from Jones & Rapport, 1997; Raab & Dunst, 1997; Wolery, et al, 1999.

ECRII Administrator's Guide

Chapter Four

Collaboration

Collaboration:
Helping Staff Work Together in Preschool Inclusive Programs

> "I've really started to see this is not just the special ed teachers sticking together type of thing. There's a real camaraderie of all the related services, especially between special ed and speech . . . You know, we are all learning about what the other person is doing." -Itinerant Teacher

When children with disabilities are included in preschool programs, new adults also appear! No matter what type of service delivery model a program uses, early childhood special educators, early childhood general educators, related services professionals, and families must work together to meet the needs of individual children. Teamwork becomes a necessity. In fact, we consider collaboration to be the *cornerstone* of effective preschool inclusion. In this chapter, we provide information useful to administrators as they mediate and facilitate collaboration. First, we define collaboration and discuss different collaboration models, next we discuss the participants involved in collaboration, and finally we provide some suggestions for making collaboration work.

What is Collaboration?

Collaboration is the relationship or partnership between two or more individuals, programs, or agencies. Research has confirmed the importance of this collaborative partnership. In successful inclusion programs, administrators have identified *relationships among professionals* as a primary facilitator of inclusion. Likewise, administrators of unsuccessful inclusion programs identified the lack of relationships among professionals as a primary barrier to inclusion.

Chapter Four

From the ECRII research and the research of many others, seven factors for successful collaboration have emerged. These factors are:

- shared philosophy
- adequate time for staff communication
- joint participation in program development
- shared "ownership" of children
- role clarity
- stability in relationships
- administrative support

From the ECRII research, we also found that the needs of children with disabilities are best met when the collaboration is active and occurs between professionals from various disciplines. We saw collaboration occurring in different ways, but before describing different models of collaboration, we will provide a brief rationale for collaboration.

Benefits of Collaboration

When successful collaboration occurs, who benefits? Our research and that of others suggests that in addition to the child with a disability, the child's family and the professionals also benefit from successful collaboration. Shown in Table 1 are some benefits of successful collaboration.

BENEFITS OF COLLABORATION

For Early Childhood Classroom Teacher

- Opportunity to work with specialists and receive expert advice on working with a child with a disability
- Opportunity to participate in the IEP planning and to gain knowledge of all goals and strategies
- Child stays in class room
- Additional adult support provided in the classroom

For Itinerant Specialists

- Opportunity to work in the classroom context where trained skills will be used
- Opportunity to teach skills when a need is presented (a capture-the-teachable-moment opportunity)
- Opportunity to work with the teaching staff

For Child with Disabilities and the Family

- Opportunity for child to be assessed in a natural environment
- Opportunity for child to learn skills in environment where they will be used
- Opportunity to stay in the classroom
- Opportunity for teachers and family to view specialized learning as something that occurs during non-therapy times, in nontherapy places, and with people other than therapists

Table 1

Chapter Four

Models of Collaboration

Collaboration, also called collaborative consultation, in preschool inclusion occurs when two or more individuals partner together to plan and implement an appropriate educational program for a child with disabilities. Three collaboration models are used in preschool inclusion:

- **itinerant-consultation model**
- **team model**
- **co-teaching model**

The itinerant-consultation model and the team model are more common than the co-teaching model; however, the co-teaching model is gaining in popularity. These models are *not* mutually exclusive, and often occur together as services for young children with disabilities are planned and implemented. For clarity, we discuss them separately.

> "In our preschool office we are trying to promote the collaboration model for the purpose of meeting the child's objectives. There's no magic in the 30 minute session, skills have to be promoted on a daily basis." - Speech Language Pathologist

Itinerant-Consultation Model of Collaboration

In the itinerant model of collaboration, a special education consultant serves a caseload of children with disabilities. The itinerant consultant makes weekly or bi-weekly visits to each child's preschool and delivers services directly to the child, indirectly through the child's teachers, or through some variation of service delivery. McWilliam (1996) has suggested that the different itinerant consultation service delivery models occur on a continuum from isolated direct services to complete consultation with the child's teacher. In Table 2, we present and describe McWilliam's continuum.

CONTINUUM OF ITINERANT CONSULTATION MODELS

Collaboration

Low   High

Individual Pull-Out   Pure Consultation

Small Group Pull-Out   Individualized Within Routines

One-on-One in Class

Group Activity

- **Individual Pull-Out:** Itinerant takes child out of the classroom for one-to-one instruction

- **Small Group Pull-Out:** Itinerant takes two or more children out of the classroom for small group instruction

- **One-on-One in Class:** Itinerant goes into classroom and takes child aside to work on goals that might not be relevant to ongoing classroom activities

- **Group Activity:** Itinerant, with consent of teacher, teaches entire class or small group (in the classroom)

- **Individualized Within Routines:** Itinerant joins child in ongoing classroom routines and teaches child in that context

- **Pure Consultation:** Itinerant and teacher jointly identify needs and develop solutions; itinerant may model use of specific strategies

Table 2
Adapted from McWilliam, 1996

ECRII Administrators' Guide

As you can see, all variations of itinerant consultation models do not facilitate collaboration. In fact, when itinerant services are delivered directly to the child, as in the Individual Pull-Out, Small Group Pull-Out, and One-on-One in Class modes, collaboration between the itinerant consultant and the child's preschool teachers may never occur. Thus, it is important for administrators to ensure both the classroom teacher and itinerant specialist share information about a child's program, before services are delivered and again after services are delivered. This before-and-after-collaboration is especially critical when an itinerant specialist proposes to deliver one-to-one pull-out services. We recommend, however, that administrators discourage regular use of one-to-one pull-out itinerant services because there is no evidence suggesting such a service delivery model impacts children's development or skills. Instead, we recommend that administrators emphasize models that encourage the itinerant consultant and the preschool teacher to identify problems and develop solutions jointly.

Team Model of Collaboration

In the team model, professionals and paraprofessionals from several disciplines make up the collaboration team. Typically, team members include educators, disability specialists, and, when necessary, health care and social service representatives. In inclusive early childhood program, three team models are used.

- The multidisciplinary team model includes individuals from various disciplines who provide their services in isolation from other team members

- The interdisciplinary team model includes members from various disciplines who provide services in isolation of other members, but also share information about their role with other team members

The transdisciplinary model includes members across disciplines who work in a reciprocal fashion. Professionals teach one another the skills needed to accomplish the desired goals for the child with disabilities. For example, a physical therapist may train a parent or classroom teacher to implement specific interventions on a day-to-day basis. Ongoing assistance is provided by the team. Typically, the transdisciplinary team leader is the teacher who is responsible for integrating the team's recommendations into the ongoing classroom routine. (For more information see Bruder, 1994).

Of course, variability will exist in how team models are carried out in real programs. In all models, however, the classroom teacher, as primary implementer of a child's program, should be an integral part of the problem solving and planning activities. This does not mean, however, that the preschool teacher is the only person who should work with the child. It does mean when transdisciplinary collaboration is used, the speech-language pathologist, physical and occupational therapists, and related specialists must ensure the classroom teachers have the training and support they need to implement the specialized procedures on a day-to-day basis.

Co-Teaching Model of Collaboration

Co-teaching has been defined as two teachers planning and delivering instruction. In our ECRII research, we found various co-teaching arrangements in which early childhood teachers and early childhood special education teachers combined their expertise and formed a partnership. Thus, we believe co-teaching is a viable option for preschool inclusion, and three of the collaborative consultation models described earlier (Group Activity, Individualized Within Routines, and Pure Consultation; see Table 2) suggest co-teaching arrangements. The literature describing co-teaching in elementary school programs is quite large. In Table 3, we present five models of co-teaching for school age populations. Although not de-

Chapter Four

veloped specifically for preschool programs, we present these models because they can be adapted easily to early childhood classrooms.

MODELS OF COLLABORATIVE CO-TEACHING

<u>One Group; One Activity</u>

· One lead teacher, and one teacher moving about providing assistance to individual children

<u>Two Groups; Two Activities</u>

· Each teacher works with a small group so children have more opportunity for engagement

<u>Two Groups; Two Activities</u>

· Each teacher works with a group of children on specified activities

<u>One Group; Multiple Activities</u>

· One teacher works with one child or a small group of children and the other teacher monitors and provides necessary support to ensure all children are appropriately engaged at activity centers

<u>No Groups; Multiple Activities</u>

· Both teachers monitor and provide necessary support to ensure all children are appropriately engaged at activity centers

---

Table 3.
Adapted from Vaughn, Schumm, and Arguelles, 1997

The goal of co-teaching arrangements is to have both teachers share equally in the implementation of a child's IEP, however, this does not occur easily. For children with disabilities, the educational program is driven by IDEA and individualized goals are formalized into an IEP. The differences between early childhood education and early childhood special education are likely to be highlighted in a co-teaching arrangement and these differences will need to be resolved before co-teaching can work effectively. In a later section of this chapter we discuss how to facilitate effective co-teaching.

Facilitating the Collaboration Environment

Our research and the research of others provides us with a lot of information about collaboration and collaboration models. Different collaboration models can be used in different programs. Components of both consultation and co-teaching collaboration models can be combined. Although team models may work best when a child's needs are severe and several specialists are involved, co-teaching strategies also can be used. In programs where both early childhood and early childhood special education teachers work with the children, co-teaching is more likely to be effective. Deciding which collaboration models to use should be determined by child needs and the number of teachers and specialists involved in the child's IEP. Before making decisions around collaboration models, however, we recommend ensuring some environmental supports for collaboration. Some program characteristics that we believe facilitate collaboration efforts are:

- A variety of child assessment information used to identify high-priority goals for children with disabilities

- A classroom program that is developmentally appropriate

- A classroom schedule that provides opportunities for children with disabilities to practice and learn their high-priority goals

· Classroom activities in which children with disabilities can participate independently or with minimal support

· Classroom staff who use specialized instructional strategies for facilitating the learning and engagement of the children with disabilities

· A system to monitor the learning and development of children with disabilities

As you probably see, these markers actually suggest high-quality inclusion. As we continue to discuss collaboration, we are reminded that when inclusion exists, collaboration must exist. Thus, if quality inclusion is a goal, then quality collaboration also is a goal.

Administrative Support of Collaboration

We recognize that administrators wear many hats. In fact, administrators have told us they could provide more support for inclusion if they did not have so many responsibilities. We also recognize that some early childhood administrators are not trained as special educators, and thus may be limited in the type of support they can provide. Nevertheless, our research and that of others continually tells us that administrative support is a primary facilitator to successful inclusion and lack of administrative support is a primary barrier to successful inclusion. Likewise, successful collaboration has been found to facilitate successful inclusion while lack of collaboration poses a barrier.

Administrative Support for the Itinerant-Consultation Model of Collaboration

Most special service providers (e.g., speech language pathologist, physical therapist, occupational therapist) who work in early childhood inclusive preschools, deliver services through an itinerant model. Similarly, many early childhood special education teachers deliver their services using an itinerant model. Typically, itinerant specialists visit a child with disabilities once or twice a week in the early childhood program. As shown in Table 2, itinerant services range from segregated pull-out to full-inclusion with full consultation. Although research does not favor any specific itinerant model of specialized service delivery, we believe the integrated models of itinerant services are more developmentally appropriate for young children with disabilities. Likewise, early childhood professionals have told us they prefer the integrated models because of the collaborative opportunities.

> "I usually do a language activity with the entire class, or sometimes with a small group including Shelly. This way, I can help everyone expand and develop language and particularly help Shelly participate more readily. Then I also leave a follow-up activity for the teacher to implement. The trick with Shelly is bringing those skills out--she needs to practice using them more." -Speech Therapist

Extensive research around collaboration between early childhood classroom teachers and itinerant specialists suggests that administrative support ranges from understanding and managing the financial constraints brought on by inclusion to monitoring activities in the classroom (McWilliam, 1996). In this section on administrative support we draw heavily from McWilliam's work. The first two areas of administrative support apply specifically to itinerant therapists. The remaining areas apply to itinerant therapists as well as to itinerant early childhood special education teachers.

Chapter Four

Financial Support for the Co-Teaching Model of Collaboration

- Hire therapists rather than contract for services

- Learn what is covered by Medicaid or other third-party insurance providers for direct and indirect services

- Learn about limits on third-party reimbursements

- Help therapists interpret direct service in the most flexible light, so they receive maximum reimbursement while maintaining their indirect service responsibilities

Amount-of-Time Issue for Itinerant Therapists

- Do not focus only on direct service but establish guidelines for indirect service, planning, and consultation time

- Do not blindly accept recommendations for therapy, but ask referral sources to specify only areas of need

- Conduct your own assessment of child and family needs

- Do not base eligibility for specialized services on a discrepancy formula; If your system does not have a method for waiving discrepancy criteria, pursue such a waiver!

- Establish policies that require staff and families to jointly review what the child needs to be successful in home and school routines

- Ensure that families understand that time spent planning and consulting with their child's teachers can be as beneficial to the child as direct service

- Have specialists apply their expertise into classroom routines

- Have teachers incorporate specialized interventions within their classroom routines

Monitor the balance of power between teachers and specialists so neither dominates the relationship

Planning for Collaborative Consultation

Ensure classroom teachers follow a daily schedule and lesson plans so specialists can plan how they will deliver their services

Ensure specialists and teachers each understand their roles, responsibilities, and expectations

Ensure interventions are functional and that teachers and therapists can explain why a child is learning a specific skill

Ensure specialists and teachers have adequate time for reciprocal consultation and that they devise a plan to ensure consultation time is used wisely

Implementing Collaborative Consultation

Ensure practitioners realize consultation is important and should not be treated as just another add-on

Regularly observe and monitor consultation before the itinerant's visit (i.e., planning), during the visit (i.e., modeling), and after the visit (i.e., follow-up information sharing and clarification)

Ensure classroom environment is conducive for itinerant services to occur

Ensure teacher has time to observe and listen to the itinerant

Arrange for itinerant and teachers to jointly attend in-service training

Chapter Four

Evaluation of Collaborative Consultation

- Devise a system to monitor what goals are addressed during the itinerant's visit and what service delivery models are being used (see Appendix for a sample evaluation form)

- Ensure teachers understand how and when to address high priority goals on a day-to-day basis; a goal-by-activity matrix is a useful organizer (see Chapter 3 for an example)

- Devise a schedule for teachers, itinerant specialists, and parents to regularly rate both a child's independence and how frequently the child uses high-priority skills; we recommend this occur at 2-3 month intervals

Administrative Support for the Team Model of Collaboration

In addition to early childhood educators, many others may have expertise to contribute to a child's program. These include early childhood disability specialists, speech/language pathologists, physical and occupational therapy specialists, psychologists, social workers, audiologists, mobility specialists, and nurses. Although the degree of contribution may vary, the goal of any early childhood collaborative team should be to enhance the outcomes for children with disabilities.

You know, bringing together a group of people does not make a collaboration team. Personalities and agendas are powerful barriers to effective team collaboration, and we realize you cannot change the personalities of team members. Administrators can, however, facilitate collaboration efforts to enhance child outcomes. With this general goal in mind, we present in Table 4 some specific goals and characteristics of early childhood collaboration teams.

GOALS AND CHARACTERISTICS OF A COLLABORATION TEAM

Goals of an Early Childhood Team

- To conduct an assessment of child and family needs and establish high priority goals and objectives

- To plan interventions for meeting the child's goals

- To implement, monitor, and evaluate planned interventions

Characteristics of Effective Collaborative Teams

- Shared philosophy

- Common goals

- Adequate meeting time

- Sharing expertise

- Effective use of collaborative skills

- Sharing the work

Characteristics of Good Collaborative Team Members

- Understands mutual support and is not protective of own turf

- Makes an effort to understand each team member's point of view

- Contributes to the team by sharing talents and knowledge

- Participates in decision making and feels ownership for goals she/he helps establish

- Understands that conflicts are normal, but works to quickly and constructively resolve any conflict

Table 4

Chapter Four

Support Toward a Shared Philosophy

The function of collaborative teams in early childhood inclusion is to assess, plan, and implement interventions that will enhance the outcomes for children with disabilities. Every inclusive program should have a stated philosophy that supports this concept of enhancing child outcomes. We provided a sample philosophy statement in Chapter 5. If your program does not have such a statement, we encourage you to develop one. If all members of the collaboration team do not share a similar philosophy, it will be difficult for the team to function optimally. As an administrator, you may identify team members who do not support your program philosophy. If this occurs, we suggest you meet individually with the team member and ask that he/she consider the benefits of inclusion and try to work cooperatively within the team. If the team member remains unsupportive of the inclusive philosophy, you may need to seek a way to replace the team member with someone who has the same expertise and also shares the team's philosophy of inclusion.

Support for Adequate Meeting Times

As you already know, the issue of meeting time is a chronic and pervasive problem. The larger the team the more difficult to schedule meetings. If the team is small, possible meeting times are before and after school or during naptime. With larger teams, it is sometimes necessary for the administrator to provide release time for participants who have child care responsibilities.

Supporting the Team to Work Toward a Common Goal

Planning a child's IEP is often the goal of a team, but the goal also may be to plan and implement a program of successful inclusion for a child. Prior to setting any time and date for a meeting, the goal for the meeting should be defined. Prior to the meeting, an agenda should be organized.

Although forms and paperwork can be viewed as unnecessary, we recommend you create a simple *Collaboration Team Agenda and Worksheet* to be used program-wide for all collaborative teams. Included on the form should be the meeting goal, team members' names, facilitator, and meeting agenda. The meeting agenda should include a statement of the team goal, a progress report if appropriate, a system for identifying new goals, and a structure for assigning task roles. A sample agenda worksheet is shown in Table 5.

Supporting Team Members to Share Their Area of Expertise

Effective transdisciplinary team collaboration requires team members to share their expertise across disciplines. This is necessary for the team to develop a successful intervention plan. This sharing of expertise requires team members to work together as both teacher and learner. Often professionals will provide training to another team member who will then deliver the service. As an administrator, you can facilitate this sharing of expertise by ensuring that the expectations of roles and responsibilities are defined and understood by all team members.

Supporting Teams Members to Use Collaborative Skills Effectively

Effective use of collaborative skills is noticed when teams accomplish their purpose of developing and implementing a program that enhances the outcomes for a young child with disabilities. As team members from each discipline begin to share their assessment information and make programming recommendations, however, logistical difficulties and philosophical differences may arise. When this occurs, the team facilitator should be prepared to guide the team through problem-solving techniques. Should your program encounter severe group conflict that requires an intervention, we recommend you seek outside help. For the smaller problems, we offer some rather simple problem-solving techniques.

Chapter Four

Collaboration Team Agenda and Worksheet

Date _____ Facilitator _____

Recorder _____ Time Keeper _____

Agenda Items

1.

2.

3.

4.

5.

Team Planning Worksheet

Problem:

Solution:

Task Analysis:

Person Responsible:

Completion Date:

Outcome:

Table 5

Adapted from Friend & Cook, 1996 ; Thousand & Villa, 1992

Problem Solving Techniques

- Identify the problem

- Find the facts, list the facts, sort the facts, organize the facts, and state the facts

- State or restate the problem

- Brainstorm solutions, list ideas, BUT defer judgement!

- Identify most promising solutions or combinations of solutions and judge them against the stated problem

- Select a solution

- Devise a step-by-step action plan for the solution

Supporting Team Members to Share the Work

Although assessment, intervention planning, and intervention implementation are functions of the entire team, the roles of individual team members vary. The day-to-day implementation of a child's program is almost always carried out by the preschool teacher. Other team members may regularly participate as itinerant specialists, while others may see the child on a yearly basis when an assessment is necessary. Whatever the level of involvement in program implementation, team members should be available to answer questions and offer new ideas. Likewise, team members who serve in an indirect capacity should visit the preschool program occasionally to show their commitment to the child and the team. As an administrator, you will want to ensure all team members understand their roles and know what others are expecting from them. Often, a little administrative push, a lot of administrative praise, and plenty of appreciation is all that it takes to ensure team members share in the work.

Chapter Four

Administrative Support for the Co-Teaching Collaboration Model

Co-teaching in early childhood programs is a model that presents a lot of promise for inclusion. Co-teaching allows the early childhood teacher and the early childhood special education teacher to combine their expertise to meet the needs of all students. In ECRII's research, we observed some creative ways administrators encouraged co-teaching within their programs. Before we begin with some suggestions, however, we share what one administrator told us about earlier failures at encouraging inclusion.

> "It was too much too fast. Teachers had some interpersonal difficulties getting along with one another. It wasn't the most positive experience! In hindsight, I would say I tried to push inclusion too soon, and some of the people I paired were not strong enough for this. But I don't regret having done it, and we'll try it again."
> - Program Administrator

Co-teaching requires both teachers to share a commitment to the collaboration process. Our experience and that of others suggests that the single most important factor in successful co-teaching is communication between the teachers. We suggest you begin with teachers who have indicated a willingness and desire to work together in a co-teaching arrangement. One administrator initiated the co-teaching project by pairing a class of preschool children with disabilities and a pre-kindergarten Head Start. No plan was specified beyond the pairing arrangement, although teachers were told their classes were expected to participate in some activities together, to celebrate birthdays together, to attend assemblies together, and to take a joint field trip. Clearly, this was not enough administrative support for the co-teaching model to be a success. In Table 7, we present a plan to help you facilitate co-teaching rather than just get it started.

The single most important factor in successful co-teaching is communication between the teachers

ACTION PLAN TO FACILITATE CO-TEACHING

Step 1

- Identify teachers who are willing to participate in a co-teaching project

Step 2

- Help teachers develop an Action Plan that includes

   Teaching and planning schedules

   Classroom management plan

   Space and classroom organization plan

   Responsibility plan (i.e., agreement about who is responsible
    for typically developing children and children with disabilities)

   Conflict resolution plan

   Role clarification

   Parental notification plan

   Evaluation plan

Step 3

- Make co-teaching a priority

Step 4

- Provide regular planning time

Step 5

- Evaluate

Step 6

- Share the successful experiences and encourage
   others to consider co-teaching

Table 7.
Adapted from Vaughn et al., 1997

Chapter Four

Summary

We stated at the beginning of this chapter our recognition that administrators wear many hats and that becoming a collaboration facilitator for your inclusive preschool program may seem like one more impossible hat to wear. We do, however, believe that a strong commitment to inclusion necessitates a strong commitment to collaboration, and thus collaboration is really just a feather in the inclusion hat. Certainly, collaboration occurs outside early childhood inclusion, but successful early childhood inclusion does not occur without successful collaboration. Our hope is that we have provided some supports to help you put the new feather in your inclusion hat.

Collaboration

Itinerant Specialists Session Form

Child _____   Date _____   Session Length (min.) _____

Specialist* _____   (circle)   SE   SLP   PT   OT   Other _____

Service delivery **   (circle)   IP/O   SGP/O   1:1C   GA   IWR   Con

Goal #	Goal	Goal Assessed	Collaboration Contact
		Yes / No	
		Yes / No	
		Yes / No	
		Yes / No	
		Yes / No	
		Yes / No	

* SE= special educator; SLP= speech language pathologist; PT= physical therapist; OT= occupational therapist

** IP/O– individual pull-out; SGP/0= small group pull-out; 1:1C= 1:1 in classroom; GA= group activity; IWR= individual within routine; Con= consultation

Adapted from McWilliam, 1996

Recommended Readings

Noonan, M. J., & McCormick, L. (2000). Practices of co teachers in inclusive preschool classrooms. *NHSA Dialog, 3,* 258-271.

Pugach, M. C., & Johnson, L. J. (1995). *Collaborative practitioners, collaborative schools.* Denver: Love Publishing.

Thousaand, J. S. & Villa, R. A. (1992). *Collaborative teams: A powerful tool in school restructuring.* In R. A. Villa, J. S. Thousaand, W. Stainback, & S. B. Stainback, *Restructuring for caring and effective education: An administrative guide to creating heterogeneous schools.* Baltimore: Paul Brookes Publishing Co.

Chapter Five

Staff Development

Staff Development:
Preparing Staff for Preschool Inclusion

Providing optimal services for young children with disabilities and their families requires support and commitment at the administrative level as well as competence and commitment at the service delivery level. It is well known that many early childhood providers in inclusive programs feel ill prepared to meet the needs of young children with disabilities. As an administrator, you probably feel responsible for providing the much needed staff development opportunities to care givers who are including children with disabilities. The purpose of this chapter is to provide some suggestions for planning and providing effective staff development. We begin the chapter with some basic information and considerations about staff development. Then, we provide an action plan to guide you in planning, implementing, and evaluating your staff development program.

Why is Staff Development Important?

Legislative initiatives and recommended practices do not ensure that optimal services for children with disabilities and their families will occur. Service providers need to have knowledge in many areas related to inclusion, and they must apply their knowledge to their particular setting. An effective staff development program can facilitate the continuous improvement of services being delivered to young children with disabilities in inclusive preschool programs. Thus, the basic goal of your staff development program should be for participants to acquire new knowledge and apply it to their practice in such a way that services for children with disabilities are improved.

There are a variety of methods for providing effective staff development. At a minimum, all service providers in your program should have two or three clearly defined and easily measured yearly goals which are monitored and evaluated regularly. In addition, yearly staff development activities for specific groups of participants should be provided. The guidelines we provide in this chapter are for group staff development activities; however, you will see that the same principles apply for individual plans as well.

Effective and Not-So-Effective Staff Development

Several years ago, researchers in Louisiana (see Sexton et al., 1996) questioned nearly 250 early intervention service providers about their experiences with inservice training and their perceptions about the effectiveness of inservice models. Not surprisingly, the care givers noted that inservice models requiring *passive* participation were unlikely to result in changes of practice. Conversely, they indicated inservice methods that included *active* participation along with *follow-up support* were most likely to result in practice changes. Table 1 provides a summary of these findings, which we believe highlight some basic considerations for planning effective staff development.

Considerations for Adult Learning and Instruction

Although the focus of staff development should be child learning, the needs and readiness-to-learn of adult participants must also be considered. In recent years, much has been written about adult learning. In Table 2, we show some basic principles of adult learning and instruction that are drawn from our own research and that of many others.

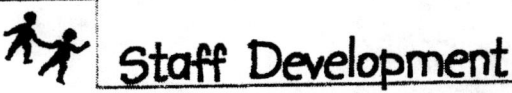 **Staff Development**

PERCEPTIONS OF INSERVICE ACTIVITIES

Ineffective

- Handouts
- Lectures
- Videos or movies

Least Likely to Result in Change of Practices

- Filling out self-revealing inventories
- Trainer provided resources
- Follow-up reminders
- Back-home plans (writing what you will do as a result of training)
- Panel discussions

Most Likely to Result in Change of Practices

- Live observations of practices being implemented
- Small-group discussions
- Demonstrations or modeling by trainer
- On-the-job follow-up assistance
- Microteaching (video-taping of trainee implementing a practice)

Table 1 adapted from Sexton, et al., 1996

Chapter Five

PRINCIPLES OF ADULT LEARNING & INSTRUCTION

· Adult learners need to understand the benefits of learning new skills

· Adult learners want to have ownership of (i.e., be responsible for) what they are learning

· Adult learners bring wide and varied experiences (both positive and negative) to the training situation

· Adult learners value learning opportunities directed at their real world and day-to-day needs and interests

· Instructional benefits and participant expectations should be clearly presented prior to initial training opportunities

· Instructional environment should facilitate active participation in the learning process

· Instructional content should be based in the expressed needs and interests of the participants

· Instructional objectives for each participant should be formally stated and agreed upon by the participant

· Trainers should encourage participants to rely on their own knowledge and experiences

· Trainees should be involved in planning and implementing evaluations of their skill acquisition and changes in practice

---

Table 2.

 Staff Development

Cautions to Consider

Staff development efforts are effective when changes in practice lead to improvement in services. The educational change movement of the 1990s has provided us with valuable information about facilitating change and about the difficulties that undermine change efforts. Our intent in this chapter is to help you facilitate programmatic changes that will lead to quality services for children with disabilities. Effective staff development is a primary means by which you can facilitate such change. Before we launch into the how-to's of effective staff development, however, we note some reasons educational change efforts have *not* been successful.

CAUSES OF CHANGE EFFORT FAILURE

- Change process was not conceptualized and the benefits of change not defined

- Change process was too broad and ambitious

- Change process was poorly supported physically and financially

- Key individuals did not have a long-term commitment to the change process

- Key individuals were controlling and/or over-committed and excluded others from the change process

- Parents were excluded from the change process

- Leadership cashed-in on early successes and moved on to other interests

---

Table 3 adapted from Hargreaves, 1997

Chapter Five

Facilitating Effective Staff Development

Although staff development can exist when one individual plans and implements a professional improvement plan, most staff development involves several individuals learning together. The staff development action plan we suggest is designed to facilitate group delivery, although the principles apply for individual staff development as well. This action plan (displayed in Table 4) is based on our own work and the work of several of our colleagues, especially Pat Trohanis of the National Early Childhood Technical Assistance Center (NEC*TAS).

ACTION PLAN FOR EFFECTIVE STAFF DEVELOPMENT

- Step 1:   Formalize your vision for inclusion and long-range plan for staff development

- Step 2:   Enlist support of key individuals

- Step 3:   Designate a coordinator

- Step 4:   Identify participants

- Step 5:   Select a planning team

- Step 6:   Conduct a needs assessment and specify the content

- Step 7:   Define training goals and expected outcomes

- Step 8:   Identify the delivery model and learning structure

- Step 9:   Address the details

- Step 10:   Implement, Evaluate, and Follow-Up

Table 4 adapted from Trohanis, 1994

ECRII Administrator's Guide

Step 1: Formalize Your Vision for Inclusion and Long-Range Plan for Staff Development

It is important for your program to have a stated vision for inclusion. A written statement, expressing your program's commitment to inclusion, is a necessary first step in planning effective staff development. It is equally important for you, as an administrator, to formalize your personal vision for inclusion. If you have never articulated this vision, we encourage you to begin by stating your vision in writing. Having defined your own vision statement will help you facilitate formalizing your program's vision statement. Although your personal vision may well be the same vision adopted by your program, it is obviously important that your program staff be involved in the process of developing the program's vision. Because this vision needs to be included in the program philosophy statement, we recommend initiating a process for revising the program philosophy. We offer some suggestions to assist in this process.

Facilitating Development of a Program Philosophy

- Recruit or solicit a staff committee willing to develop a program philosophy statement

- Solicit input from staff around individual visions for inclusion to be included in the program philosophy statement

- Share philosophy statements from other inclusive programs so the philosophy committee will have models (See Table 5 for an example)

Your program's philosophy statement, of course, will not ensure unanimous endorsement of inclusion, but it will serve to articulate the program's commitment to providing inclusive services for children with disabilities. Furthermore, a clearly articulated statement of your vision for inclusion will help formalize your long-term staff development plan. Using your vision statement to represent the ideal, you can identify areas most in need of change. This, in turn, will allow you to prioritize the needs for a long-range staff development plan. Remember, however, overly ambitious change efforts are typically not successful. Thus, you will likely need to extend the long-range plan over several years.

Step 2: Enlist the Support of Key Individuals

Depending on how inclusive services are supported in your program and through your own administrative responsibilities, you will need to identify some key individuals to support your staff development efforts. These individuals may be from the local ICC, university, or state EC division. Having the support of key individuals may ensure that your efforts toward staff development are viewed as credible and important, and could increase the potential for financial and other resource support.

Step 3: Designate a Coordinator

Perhaps this is you, but it is important for one person to be responsible for the organization and follow-through of all staff development activities.

Step 4: Select a Planning Team

An effective planning team should include representatives from the various participant groups (i.e., teachers, teaching assistants, specialists). This team will assist the coordinator in planning and organizing the staff development program. You will likely have a new planning team each year; however, it may be useful to rotate team members so you can take advantage of experience.

Step 5: Identify Participants

All early childhood educators in your program should participate in yearly staff development efforts; although the participants and the intensity may differ from year to year. One year you may want to direct much of your staff development effort to a specific audience such as preschool teach-

SAMPLE PHILOSOPHY STATEMENT

Inclusion is about community, about membership, about relationships, and about development. The goal of the classroom programs at the Experimental Education Unit is to provide a positive educational experience to children with diverse abilities in a setting that enhances the strengths, and supports the needs, of all children in our program; and provides children with opportunities to build memberships, establish relationships, and develop functional skills.

The goal of our program is to enhance the competence and confidence of the children and families with whom we work. Our program is committed to providing children with opportunities to learn communication skills, to develop social relationships, and to learn other functional skills in an integrated, developmentally appropriate classroom. Families are involved in identifying the priority skills for their child and are encouraged to take an active role in the classroom.

A goal of our program is to promote active social integration between children with and without disabilities across all parts of the school day. Effective and systematic assessment and instructional strategies are used to identify, teach, and support these important skills. Skills are taught within the context of meaningful activities across the classroom curriculum. Support services (e.g., speech therapy, occupational therapy, and physical therapy) are provided in naturalistic settings (i.e., the classroom) and use activity-based instruction to enhance skill acquisition and generalization. Data are collected to monitor child progress and instructional decisions are based on those data.

Used with permission from the Experimental Education Unit (EEU),
University of Washington, Seattle.

Table 5

Chapter Five

Staff development activities also can be a major component of the yearly staff evaluation program

ers, teaching assistants, or itinerant service providers. Another year, you may want to direct staff development efforts towards the entire staff. When the planning team develops long-range goals for your program, it should also identify the target audience for specific staff development efforts. Remember, however, all efforts need not be directed at formalized training sessions and activities. Staff development activities also can be a major component of the yearly staff evaluation program.

Step 6: Conduct a Needs and Interest Assessment and Identify the Content

You may be tempted to skip this step because you've heard it over and over: "We need to know how to facilitate the inclusion of young children with disabilities." There are many reasons, however, to conduct a needs and interest assessment. For example:

- **A needs and interest assessment can facilitate the feeling of ownership in the staff development process**

- **The needs and interest assessment instrument will provide staff with an outline of the content areas you want them to consider important**

- **A needs and interest assessment provides you with information about your staff's perceptions of the importance of various components of inclusion**

Ideally, areas of staff development will be identified through the needs and interest assessment. Sometimes, however, a content area may be identified. For example, a state agency may require specific training, or recently enacted legislation may necessitate specific training. Nevertheless, it is important to specify clearly how the content of staff development will serve to facilitate success in meeting both individual and program

 Staff Development

goals and outcomes.

In this chapter's appendix, we provide a sample needs assessment instrument. This needs assessment is based on inservice topics used in the University of Connecticut's Training for Inclusion Project (Bruder, 1998). We encourage you to use this form or develop a similar instrument so your staff can identify specific staff development interests and needs.

Step 7: Define Training Goals and Expected Outcomes

As we noted earlier, the *basic* goal of your staff development efforts should be to facilitate changes in practice that lead to improved services for children with disabilities. Initially, however, the *specific* goals and expected outcomes of your staff development efforts must be identified. Defining the goals and expected outcomes of your staff development efforts will facilitate not only the implementation of your training efforts but also the follow-up and evaluation efforts. In addition, your goal and outcome statements can provide you with documentation of the effectiveness of the staff development program.

Goals and outcomes should be written as statements that identify clearly the changes you hope to see. This applies to changes at both the program level and at the individual level. Keep in mind, however, that inservice participants should not perceive the goal and outcome statements as simply a back-home plan (i.e., what they will do after training). Rather, participants should view the goal and outcome statements as a practical and functional means of defining what they plan to learn and how they plan to apply their new knowledge.

If you have developed a vision for inclusion statement, you implicitly identified the goals and outcomes for your program. Before you begin formal staff development training, however, you may want to formulate those goals and outcomes into statements that can be shared with your staff.

You also may want to present annual goal and outcome statements at the beginning of each school year, or at the onset of yearly staff development training efforts. Such statements clarify your vision and commitment to an inclusive program and can serve as a model for participants to follow in developing their individual goal and outcome statements. It is very important that goal and outcome statements describe the *practices* that change, not just the knowledge that causes the change. We can not observe knowledge or understanding; but, we can observe practices that indicate an application of knowledge and understanding. Thus, goal and outcome statements should specify how the knowledge will be applied, that is, the practice. Shown in Table 6 are sample goal and outcome statements.

SAMPLE GOAL/OUTCOME STATEMENTS - PROGRAM LEVEL

Outcome 1 : To become an inclusive preschool program.

· Goal (this year): To increase the percentage of children with disabilities in our program from 5% to 20%.

Outcome 2: To provide specialized instruction for all children with disabilities included in our program.

· Goal 1 (this year): For each child with disabilities, the preschool teacher will target at least *one* IEP goal *each* week and plan purposeful activities that provide *daily* teaching and learning opportunities toward the targeted IEP goal.

· Goal 2 (this year): For each targeted IEP goal, the teacher will develop a recording system that states targeted goal, identifies activity used to facilitate child learning, and child response to teaching and learning opportunity.

· Goal 3 (this year): To meet with teachers at least one time every 8 weeks to evaluate the specialized instructional plan.

Table 6

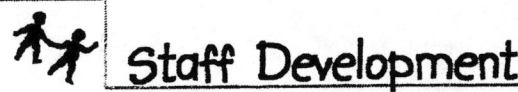 Staff Development

Step 8: Identify the Delivery Model and Learning Structure

There are numerous models for delivering staff development. When selecting a model of delivery, factors such as time, resources, and content are important. Your planning team should provide input on which models will best facilitate the participant audience. Here are some examples of such models:

- In-school workshops

- Off-site workshops

- Conferences, institutes, or courses

- Visits to other programs

- Consultants

- Media presentations

- Small group work sessions

A learning structure is the philosophical support for the delivery model. Organizing your staff development around a sound learning structure can ensure the participants have opportunity to acquire the information you are presenting. At the beginning of this chapter, we presented some research findings that pointed to effective and not so effective inservice strategies. The consensus from that research was that active audience participation and follow-up support are inservice strategies most likely to facilitate practice change. Several learning structures have been described, however, we like Verduin, Miller, and Greer's four-phase model described by Trohanis (1994). This simple structure is consistent with the research findings mentioned earlier.

FOUR-PHASE LEARNING STRUCTURE FOR STAFF DEVELOPMENT

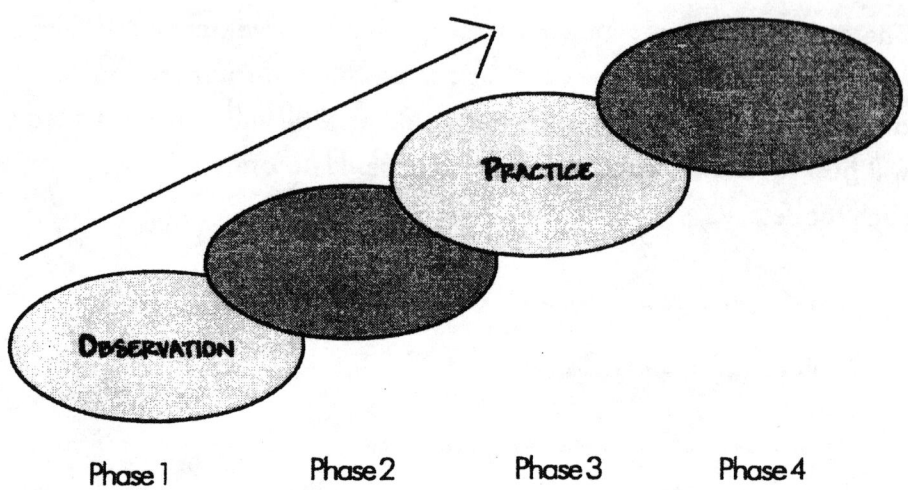

Phase 1	Phase 2	Phase 3	Phase 4

This four-phase learning structure can be used with group and individualized staff development. For example, in Phase 1, a large group training might begin with an introduction to the content and a video presentation showing how the information is applied. Phase 2 would follow with small group sessions in which participants role play and practice applying the new information while a trainer is present to facilitate. Phase 3 would occur when participants return to their programs and practice applying their new knowledge with support and follow-up from trainers or mentors. Finally, Phase 4 occurs when application of the new knowledge becomes a part of the participant's skill and knowledge repertoire.

For individual staff development, a staff member might plan an inservice component which begins with observations of a mentor teacher (Phase 1). This would be followed by an imitation session in the presence of the mentor (Phase 2), and then classroom practice with support from the mentor (Phase 3). Adoption of the new skills (Phase 4) would finalize the inservice.

Step 9: Address the Details

Many details arise when planning staff development activities. Some details relate to logistics such as dates, time, location, room arrangement, and grouping. Other details to consider relate to resources and finances. What print and AV materials are needed and how will they be provided? Are there financial resources for consultant fees? Who is responsible for handouts and printing? What about mailings and postage? To maximize your efforts and those of the planning team, we suggest someone be assigned the task of maintaining a checklist of all the detail items. As new detail items surface, they are added to the list. From this list, the inservice coordinator can monitor the progress toward addressing the details.

Another detail deserving consideration is incentives. Will staff receive any compensation for their efforts? Are continuing education credits or tuition options available? Is comp-time or flextime an option? Can staff attend off-site training during work time?

Step 10: Implement, Evaluate, and Follow-Up

Implementation. As with most other educational efforts, planning is the hardest part! If your planning efforts have been successful, however, initial implementation of your staff development activities should proceed smoothly.

Evaluation. Two types of evaluation are important and should be part of your staff development. First, you want to solicit evaluation *feedback* from participants related to the content and logistics of the presentation. Such feedback will inform future planning. A brief questionnaire can be developed for participants to rate or comment on their perceptions of the appropriateness, usefulness, and applicability of the training.

Chapter Five

The second type of evaluation is more extensive. This type of evaluation should inform you with evidence that participants took the information you provided and applied it in ways that facilitate improved services for children with disabilities. We are not suggesting a comprehensive pre- and post-evaluation to determine if participants learned what was taught, but rather a system to identify and evaluate changes in practice. If you adopt a learning structure that includes a method of follow-up support, you can devise some rather simple record-keeping procedures for this kind of evaluation. Of course, you are not likely to be the sole individual providing follow-up support, so other monitoring and evaluation options will need to be devised. Ideally, you can observe each teacher several times a year and evaluate progress on staff development goals during observation visits. As we have stated before, we know administrators have many responsibilities. Nevertheless, we encourage you to consider the importance of follow-up evaluation related to staff development.

Follow-up. We have already discussed follow-up as a method of evaluation. Different from the follow-up evaluation, however, is follow-up as a part of ongoing staff development. As mentioned previously, research suggests that staff development participants perceive follow-up support as facilitating their ability to apply new knowledge to their practice. All staff development efforts need to include some type of useful follow-up support. Individual and program goals are not met when the inservice session ends. Practice is an important part of change process, and goals are met when practice becomes adoption. Participants need to know their efforts to change are noticed. Perhaps members of the planning team can assume some responsibility for follow-up support. Mentor teachers and consultants also can provide follow-up support. Whatever method of inservice you use, follow-up support is not a component to eliminate.

research suggests that follow-up support facilitates participants' ability to apply new knowledge to their practice.

 Staff Development

Summary

High quality staff development can lead to high quality services. It also can lead to a better working environment and higher retention of competent staff. Your staff development efforts will likely be shaped by a combination of factors that include, but are not limited to, your personal vision for inclusion, the goals toward inclusion that exist in your community, the attitudes and interests of the service providers in your program, the expectations of family members, and the range of children with disabilities in your program. In this chapter, we have provided an action plan to assist you in developing quality staff development. Just as we encourage inclusive preschool teachers to make adaptations and modifications to the classroom environment and curriculum, we encourage you to make adaptations and modifications to this action plan for staff development. We also encourage your efforts in providing quality staff development as a means of delivering optimal services to children with disabilities in an inclusive preschool program.

> "You know, teachers are good and caring people, but they are not always trained to do all of those specialized things. We need more training on how to do assessments, on how to manage data collection, actually, we need training on the whole service delivery thing." - Preschool teacher

Chapter Five

Inservice Needs and Interest Inventory

Please check the priority level (High, Moderate, Low) for each inservice topic according to your current needs. Please check any sub-topics that indicate a specific area of interest.

Topic 1: Inclusion and the Individuals With Disabilities Act (IDEA)

☐ High Priority ☐ Moderate Priority ☐ Low Priority

_____ Defining young children with disabilities.

_____ Defining inclusion

_____ Understanding the rationale for including children with disabilities into programs with typically developing children

_____ Understanding the benefits of inclusion for children, families, and providers

_____ Characteristics of an effective inclusive early childhood program

_____ Understanding the laws relating to inclusion

_____ Understanding how the Americans with Disabilities Act (ADA) impacts early childhood programs

_____ Understanding the rights of children with disabilities

Topic 2: Building Partnerships with Families

☐ High Priority ☐ Moderate Priority ☐ Low Priority

_____ Defining a family and a family system

_____ Defining cultural sensitivity

_____ Designing a program to include diversity

_____ Knowing how a child with a disability affects a family

_____ Defining family-centered services

_____ Building partnerships with families

Staff Development

Topic 3: Identifying Young Children with Special Needs

☐ High Priority   ☐ Moderate Priority   ☐ Low Priority

_____ Understanding child development and developmental milestones

_____ Identifying children who may have developmental delays or disabilities

_____ Understanding screening instruments

_____ Approaching parents with concerns about their child

_____ Knowing what happens to a child after screening

_____ Knowing how to conduct assessments

_____ Knowing what should happen after a child is determined eligible for services

Topic 4: What is an IFSP and IEP?

☐ High Priority   ☐ Moderate Priority   ☐ Low Priority

_____ Understanding IFSPs and IEPs

_____ Knowing what information should be included on IFSPs and IEPs

_____ Knowing who should be involved in developing IFSPs and IEPs and their roles

_____ Understanding the IFSP and IEP process

_____ Understanding goals and objectives

_____ Understanding collaborative goal setting

_____ Knowing what constitutes a successful IFSP or IEP

Topic 5: Implementing Interventions into Daily Routines

☐ High Priority   ☐ Moderate Priority   ☐ Low Priority

_____ Understanding why interventions should be implemented during daily routines

_____ Understanding a naturalistic curriculum

_____ Determining what children with disabilities need to learn

Chapter Five

_____ Arranging the environment to facilitate the teaching and learning process

_____ Selecting appropriate materials for children with disabilities

_____ Monitoring and evaluating the teaching and learning process

_____ Knowing instructional strategies for accommodating the needs of children with disabilities

_____ Understanding material and curriculum adaptations to accommodate the needs of children with disabilities

_____ Understanding assistive technology

_____ Understanding the importance of environmental designs in the teaching and learning process

_____ Knowing how to schedule and organize daily activities

_____ Planning specific learning activities and play areas

_____ Promoting motor development

_____ Promoting social competence

_____ Promoting self-help skills

_____ Promoting communication and language development

_____ Promoting early literacy development

_____ Knowing how to evaluate a child's progress

_____ Understanding the principles of behavior management.

Topic 6: Collaborating with Others

☐ High Priority   ☐ Moderate Priority   ☐ Low Priority

_____ Understanding collaboration

_____ Knowing why collaboration is important

_____ Knowing who should be involved in collaboration

_____ Knowing how to collaborate

_____ Understanding collaborative service delivery teams

_____ Understanding the team process

_____ Knowing strategies early childhood providers use to ensure collaboration

 **Staff Development**

Topic 7: The Inclusive Early Childhood Program

☐ High Priority   ☐ Moderate Priority   ☐ Low Priority

_____ Understanding an inclusive early childhood program

_____ Knowing the importance of program goals

_____ Knowing the purpose of program goals and objectives

_____ Knowing the importance of staff development as a program goal

_____ Understanding how to provide learning opportunities to staff in an inclusive early childhood program

_____ Knowing how an inclusive program can be certain it is accessible and meets the needs of children and families

_____ Knowing how to conduct program evaluations

Additional Comments or Suggestions:

Adapted from Bruder, 1998

Chapter Six

Costs and Financing

Costs and Financing
Considering the Costs of Preschool Inclusion

In an ideal world, the cost of services should not influence decisions about the provision of services, but few of us live in an ideal world. Although child needs and family priorities should be the guiding factors when educational services for preschool children with disabilities are planned, it is often not the case. In our study of barriers to preschool inclusion, we found that teachers, administrators, and coordinators repeatedly identified costs and financing as primary factors in decision making. In fact, one administrator, when asked to write his definition of inclusion wrote, "Inclusion is $$$." Moreover, among some administrators, we found a perception that inclusive preschool programs are more costly than traditional self-contained special education programs.

> "The funding formula for preschool inclusion programs remains problematic . . . you have to pay for the opportunity to put this child with normally developing children and it is just financially more punitive." - System level Administrator

Cost of Preschool Inclusion: Does it Cost More?

Because little information about the cost of preschool inclusion exists, ECRII investigators began an investigation of specific costs related to classroom instruction, specialized services, and specialized equipment. We conducted this study in local education agencies (LEAs) in five different states across the country (Odom, et al; 2000). Programs represented seven different inclusion contexts and the traditional self-contained preschool program operating in each LEA (see Table 1 for program descriptions).

INCLUSION MODELS IN THE ECRII COST STUDY

Community-based / Itinerant

Programs in which an itinerant special education teacher and related services staff visited on a regular (usually weekly) basis

Head Start / Itinerant

Programs in which children were enrolled in Head Start and an itinerant special education teacher visited frequently

Public School / Co-Teaching

Programs in which an early childhood teacher and a special education teacher co-led the a public school early childhood classroom

Community-based / Co-Teaching

Programs in which early childhood and early childhood special education teachers shared teaching responsibilities

Public School Tuition Based

An inclusive early childhood program that charged tuition for typically developing; the lead teachers were certified in childhood special education

Integrated Activities

Programs in which children with and without disabilities were enrolled in different classes but came together several a week times for special activities

Traditional Special Education

Programs in which only children with disabilities were enrolled and a special education was the lead teacher

Table 1 from Odom et al., 1999

 Costs and Financing

Sometimes, preschool inclusive programs are funded through more than one source. For example, in a Head Start/co-teaching program, the Head Start agency may fund their teacher and the school system may pay for a special education teacher. For the ECRII cost study, instructional costs incurred by the school district and total instructional costs were investigated. In Table 2, cost figures for nine inclusive programs and five noninclusive special education programs are presented. *Total Instructional Costs* reflects monies contributed by all agencies and *Cost to LEA* reflects only instructional cost paid by the school system.

INSTRUCTIONAL COSTS OF PRESCHOOL INCLUSION

State	A	B	C	D	E
Special Ed (non-inclusive)					
Total Inst. cost	$3817	$3886	$5650	$4445	$1936
Cost to LEA	$3079	$3886	$4963	$4445	$1576
Community based (inclusive)					
IT* Total Inst. Cost	$2436		$4364	$4863	
IT* Cost to LEA	$1319		$1325	$4863	
CT* Total Inst. Cost				$6886	
CT* Cost to LEA				$6886	
Head Start (inclusive)					
IT* Total Inst. Cost	$4760				$1687
IT* Cost to LEA	$2151				$1687
Public School (inclusive)					
CT* Total Inst. Cost		$3297			
CT* Cost to LEA		$3297			
TB* Total Inst. Cost					$1203
TB* Cost to LEA					$941
IA* Total Inst. Cost				$2481	
IA* Cost to LEA				$2481	

* IT=Itinerant Teaching; CT=Co-Teaching; TB=Tuition-based; IA=Integrated activities

Table 2. from ECRII Cost of Preschool Inclusion Study; Odom et al., 2000

Chapter Six

As you can see from studying Table 2, costs to the LEA for inclusive services was less expensive than costs of traditional special education programs in six of the nine inclusive programs. Furthermore, in state D, the high costs incurred by the two community-based contexts were attributable to tuition fees the school district paid to the community-based programs. Our study, however, only reports instructional costs. Some important noninstructional costs such as administration, transportation, and buildings were not included in our study and we recognize the cost figures we present do not reflect the complete cost of preschool inclusion.

Although we were unable to get exact cost figures, we assume that administrative costs and building costs across both inclusive and traditional special education programs operating in the public school are fairly comparable. When inclusive classrooms operate in the community, we expect additional administrative costs are absorbed in the tuition. Likewise, building costs (i.e., maintenance, electricity, telephone) would also be absorbed in the tuition. Transportation costs, on the other hand, are likely to differ depending on the context. For example, programs using an itinerant teaching model have transportation costs that do not exist in co-teaching programs, and programs where parents provide their child's transportation do not have school bus expenses.

While the cost study allowed us to examine instructional costs in five programs, administrators should be cautious about applying these findings to their own program. In fact, we recommend that administrators who have questions about costs consider doing a simple cost analysis on their own. In the remainder of this chapter we identify different types of costs that exist for various models of inclusion and we suggest ways administrators can use this information to estimate their own program costs.

Cost Features of Inclusive Programs

Costs associated with each type of inclusive program vary depending on the program options and the needs of individual children in the program. Administrators can obtain a general idea of costs within their school district by looking at features of the specific type of inclusive programs. In Table 3, we display a matrix showing the various types of inclusive programs and various features that contribute to the cost of each program type. For discussion, we group the various cost features within the general organizational context of community-based, Head Start, and public school programs.

Community-Based Programs

When children with disabilities are enrolled in community-based programs, several features of the program contribute to costs. The LEA usually provides an itinerant teacher who visits the program to consult with the teacher and perhaps provide direct instruction to the child. Likewise, related service professionals are hired on an itinerant basis and in some cases, the LEA provides a classroom assistant. Certainly, paying salaries for several itinerants contributes significantly to the cost of inclusion.

Transportation costs, another significant budget item for all educational systems, also are cost features in the community-based context. These include travel expenses (e.g., mileage reimbursement or LEA provided vehicle) for the itinerant teacher and related service providers in addition to the cost of transporting children to and from the program. If the LEA does not provide transportation but arranges with parents to transport their children, reimbursements to parents will be a cost item.

Another a significant cost item for community-based programs is tuition. In some programs, parents pay the tuition, but in other programs the LEAs pay for an "educationally relevant" part of the child's program.

Other costs that might be incurred by the LEAs include equipment or materials to a child care program. We, however, found this to be the exception rather than the rule. In community-based programs, building costs should be minimal or non-existent, unless the itinerant teacher needs an office or workspace. Similarly, administrative costs for both community-based inclusion and self contained programs should not differ. Administrative cost at the inclusive child care center will occur, however, such costs would be embedded into the child care tuition paid by either the parents or the LEA.

Head Start Programs

The cost to LEAs for inclusive service operating in Head Start classrooms depends on whether the school system or an independent agency holds the Head Start contract. If the school system holds the contract, it is responsible for all costs of the program (See Table 3). Presumably, (although we have not analyzed this), funds received from the federal government would pay the Head Start costs, so costs to the LEA may be about the same as costs for the model in which an independent agency holds the Head Start contract.

In places where the Head Start contract is held by an independent agency, that agency usually provides the building, teachers, materials, and perhaps food. For children with disabilities in the program, we found individual negotiations sometimes occurred specifically to obtain funds for food, materials, and equipment.

Similar to the community-based model, if itinerant teachers or related service providers are used in a Head Start program, the LEA pays salary and transportation costs. The LEA also is likely to provide

Costs and Financing

MATRIX OF COST CATEGORIES

Program Costs	Community Based IT	Head Start Independent IT	Head Start School System IT	Head Start Independent CT	Public School CT	Public School IT	Traditional
Itinerant Special Education Teacher	X	X	X			X	
Early Childhood Classroom Teacher			X		X	X	
Special Education Classroom Teacher				X	X		X
Paraprofessional	*	*	X	X	X	X	X
Related Service Personnel	X	X	X	X	X	X	X
Child Care Tuition	*						
Transportation for Child	*	X	X	X	X	X	X
Transportation for Teacher	X	X	X			X	
Equipment	*	*	X	*	X	X	X
Materials			X	*	X	X	X
Building Costs			X		X	X	X
Food-Snacks			X	*	X	X	X
Administrative Costs	X	X	X	X	X	X	X

IT = Itinerant Teacher Model; CT = Co-Teacher Model

* = Cost may or may not be provided by the LEA

Table 3

Chapter Six

Successful Approach: Head Start Income Waivers

Head Start programs usually have an income waiver for a small percentage of children in their program. This waiver may be used by the program to enroll children with disabilities whose parents' income exceeds the Head Start criteria. This may be an advantage to some Head Start programs that do not meet the 10% disability mandate.

Successful Approach: Dual Enrollment

It is possible for some children with disabilities to qualify for Head Start and for special education services offered through an LEA. This duplicate funding can provide incentives for both the Head Start program and public school program to collaborate.

Successful Approach: Sliding Scale Tuition

Local, nonprofit child care programs (which often have multiple funding bases) may offer tuition fees on a "sliding-scale," which may benefit families of children with disabilities who meet the income guidelines. These child care centers can serve as inclusive sites for their children. School district staff may assist families in accessing these programs by, for example, informing them about the availability of the program and helping them complete the application, if necessary.

Successful Approach: Title I

In some school districts, federal Title I funds are used to fund programs for preschool children who might have reading problems when they enter the public schools. These preschool programs have been used as inclusive sites for children with disabilities.

 # Costs and Financing

Successful Approach: Tuition-Based Preschools

Some local school systems have opened fee-for-service preschool programs for typically developing children in the community. Parents of typically developing children pay tuition for their child to attend the program. These programs, then, can serve as inclusive sites for young children with disabilities.

Successful Approach: High School Child Care Programs

Child care centers sometimes exist in public high schools. These programs may provide child care services to staff or students and also may be used as vocational training sites. Since these programs operate fiscally within the public school system, they may be available as inclusive placements for some children with disabilities. Financing for the child care program may come from the general education budget, tuition paid by parents of the typically developing children, or some combination of both these sources.

We have highlighted a few ways in which public school administrators have found funding for inclusive preschool sites. We found, however, that both a vast assortment of funding options and enormous variability exists across different programs. As will be mentioned in the next chapter, locating inclusive sites and solving the problem of how the program will be funded for typically developing children is often a function of the creativity and flexibility of the key administrator.

Chapter Seven

Family-Centered Inclusion

Family-Centered Inclusion

Kelly is a preschooler who is blind and in enrolled in an inclusive program. Her mother told us:

> "We, my mom and me, went to the blind school for a summer preschool conference. I just don't think it is the place for Kelly. They have rails all down the hallways. Everywhere you go there is Braille, Braille, Braille . . . I like it (Kelly's inclusive preschool) because she's going to school with, well, normal kids . . . She's got a lot of interaction with kids that there's nothing wrong with them . . . She needs to learn how to get around and get along with people who can see and how to act and how to take care of herself and behave herself in public like she should . . . That's the biggest thing."

Just as inclusion has evolved as a recommended practice in the field of early childhood special education, providing services in a family-centered way also has become a highly valued practice. As Kelly's mother expressed, participation in the inclusive program is very important to their family because they believe it will prepare Kelly for life in mainstream society. Part of your role as an administrator involves listening to family concerns and desires for their children, providing them with the necessary information to make decision about services, and recognizing the diversity that exists across families. When planning services and placements for children, keeping the family at the center of the process is essential. In our research, and the research of others, family members have voiced their support for inclusion and their concerns about inclusion.

Chapter Seven

We also have learned that parents are influenced—in a major way—by their first encounters with the school system, and their ongoing interactions with administrators and program staff.

The purpose of this chapter is to discuss general themes we believe administrators should consider when they work with families of children in inclusive programs. We open this chapter with a brief description of family member's perceptions of inclusion, drawn from our own research and the research of others. We also discuss how diversity influences family concerns, families' need for information, the importance of service options, and finally, we offer some ideas for providing family support. Because much has been written in recent years detailing how family-centered services should be delivered, we do not add to that discussion. We do, however, provide some recommend readings and resources.

Family Members' Perceptions of Inclusion

Parents' perceptions of inclusion have been studied widely and the findings are relatively consistent. Some of the benefits of inclusion, identified by parents of children with disabilities are:

- Increased acceptance from others

- Increased opportunities to learn

- Availability of good developmental and behavioral models

- Preparation for the real world

- Improved self-concepts

- Positive social contacts

- Friendships with typically developing peers

- Developmental gains

 # Family-Centered Inclusion

On the other hand, parents also have expressed some concerns about inclusion. Specifically, parents have reported being concerned about:

· **Difficulty obtaining special services**

· **Difficulty obtaining individualized instruction from teachers**

· **Inadequately trained staff**

· **Large class size and staff-to-child ratios**

· **Teasing or rejection by peers**

As part of our research on barriers to and facilitators of preschool inclusion, ECRII investigators conducted studies in which family members were interviewed. Our conclusions about family perceptions of and experience with inclusion are summarized in seven points (Hanson et al., in press).

Family Summary Point 1: Perceptions about inclusion are influenced by their individual frames of reference, that is their previous experiences, goals and expectations for their child, socioeconomic status, etc.

Family Summary Point 2: Families have good experiences when there is congruence between what a program provides and what they perceive as their child's needs

Family Summary Point 3: Families often feel they have limited options and little choice about their child's program

Family Summary Point 4: Families often cannot make choices because they have limited information about inclusion, programs, and their rights

Family Summary Point 5: Access to information is influenced by factors such as socioeconomic status and culture

Chapter Seven

Family Summary Point 6: Families are often concerned about the availability of special, individualized services and class size in inclusive settings

Family Summary Point 7: Both family and professional views of a child's "readiness" influences participation in inclusive programs

Factors Affecting Family Perceptions

Family members' perspectives about their child with disabilities are influenced by a range of factors occurring in their lives. When an administrator communicates with parents about their child's program, the need to take into account these influences is paramount. In this section, we discuss some specific areas of influence that should be considered.

Cultural Influences

One of the most powerful influences of family perspective is culture. It is only natural that family views about their child's educational program are filtered through cultural lenses. For some families, not only does their value system differ from mainstream society, but their language system also is different. Understanding cultural perspectives and how they influence families wishes, desires, or advocacy for their child is a critical role for administrators of inclusive programs. Noted below are some examples of cultural and linguistic diversity that influence family decisions about and access to inclusive placements for young children with disabilities.

Cultural Beliefs About Disability and Parental Roles

The cultural influences of family perceptions of disability and their role as the parent of a child with disabilities vary considerably. In some cultures, for example, it is believed that children with disabilities are given only to parents who are capable of caring for the special needs of the child. For example a Mexican father interviewed by Skinner and her colleagues stated:

> "It's a special message from God saying you're somebody special and that you deserve this." (Skinner, Rodriiguez, & Bailey, 1999, p. 273).

In another culture, however, having a child with a disability may be viewed as a punishment; perhaps for past transgressions. Families holding this belief may be reluctant to place their child in settings outside the home or in programs with typically developing children where the child with disabilities might standout. On the other hand families with this belief might perceive their role as one of child advocate. A mother interviewed by Skinner and her colleagues illustrates this belief.

> "It's a test. . . . I accept it and I will help my son to the end, and I will demonstrate to God and to the world that I can attend him and help him and get him ahead." (Skinner et al., 1999, p. 279).

Cultural Beliefs About Authority

In some cultures, families are reluctant to challenge authority or advocate for their child, and in many cases, these values are combined with limited language and resources. Cultural influences such as these can result in some children not having the same access to inclusive placements as children from families in the mainstream culture. This is especially likely to occur in systems where inclusion, as an option, is not communicated to all parents.

Parents' Language

Even if the school district provides an interpreter, family members who speak languages other than English can be at a disadvantage when it comes to understanding and participating in meetings where decisions

Chapter Seven

about their child's placement are being made. Likewise, after the child is placed, communication between the school and the home may be a concern.

Cultural Beliefs About Inclusion

Sometimes cultural values influence beliefs about inclusion. Family members of typically developing children may feel they do not want their child around children with disabilities. A school principal related the following story.

> "We had a parent come and say, 'I don't want my child eating with this other child.' It happened to be an Asian parent—immigrant parent—talking about her child eating with a child with Down syndrome...I explained that was the ways things worked at our center but I could tell she was kind of troubled. So I asked her if she would do me a favor and come to lunch one day so she could see what happens when the children are mixed. So she came to lunch and afterwards she came to me—and I'm pretty sure she had tears in her eyes—and she told me it was all right. You know, this is powerful stuff." (Hanson et al, 1998).

The message we wish to send to administrators is that the influence of family cultural issues, as they apply to the inclusion of young children with disabilities, are multifaceted and complex. Certainly maintaining an awareness of cultural influences will make your job more challenging. But when things work well, as they did with the principal mentioned previously, your job is more enriching. If program placement decisions begin with inclusion as the first option considered, many of the concerns about cultural issues interfering with placement in inclusive settings are allayed. However, listening carefully, being sensitive to different perspectives, and empowering family members' to participate in decisions about the most appropriate program for their child always is important. For your reference, we list resources at the end of this chapter for working with families from different cultures.

Other Influences

A myriad of other factors influence family members' perceptions about inclusion. Space does not permit a detailed review of these, however, we briefly note some of the more common influences and refer you to the resource section at the end of this chapter.

The Nature of the Child's Disability

Sometimes family members, like school systems, perceive nonintegrated special education programs as more intense and therefore more appropriate placements for children with severe disabilities. This perception, however, is not supported by research. In fact, some children with severe disabilities have been shown to benefit more when placed in inclusive programs than in segregated programs.

Socioeconomic Status and Education Level (often merged)

Various studies of parent perceptions report that both family socioeconomic states and parents' education influence what families think about inclusion. Parents with more education (high school graduates and beyond) generally report more positive perceptions about inclusion than parents who did not complete high school. Likewise families in higher income groups report more positive perceptions of inclusion.

Siblings, and Others Family Members Living in the Home

Parents often view one child's development in comparison with his or her brothers and sisters. Moreover, parents may want their child with disability to have experiences similar to those of an older sibling. A family in our study, for example, wanted their child with autism to be placed in the same community-based child care center his typically developing sister attended. Another influence may come in the form of support from a large extended family living in the home.

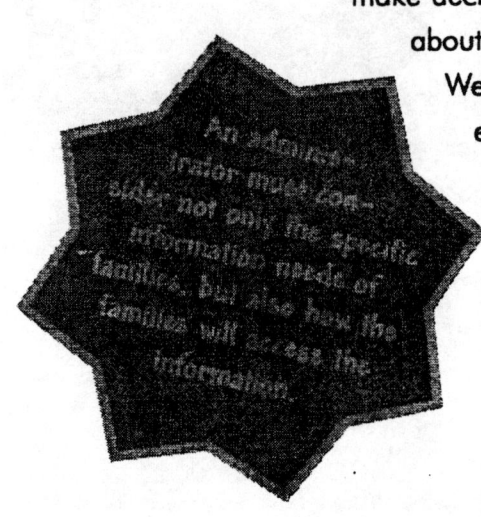

Understanding the factors that influence how families perceive their inclusion experiences, is a necessary first step in providing high-quality preschool inclusive services that are family-centered.

Clearly, there are many factors that influence how early childhood professionals interact with families. Understanding the factors that influence how families perceive their inclusion experiences, is a necessary first step in providing high-quality preschool inclusive services that are family-centered. In the next section, we discuss the families need for information.

Facilitating Family Access to Information

A second theme, noted in our research and the research of others, is that families need information. In fact, we found that families often cannot make decisions because they have limited information about inclusion, about programs, and about their rights (Family Summary Point #4). We also found that family ability to access information is influenced by factors such as socioeconomic status and culture. For example a Latino mother in our study related the following story about her experiences.

An administrator must consider not only the specific information needs of families, but also how the families will access the information.

"First, the school system make a lot of test to him and told me he was autistic. I was worried so I take him the Doctor and ask if he needed medication. The Doctor tell me my son is really not autistic boy, but he has a little problem about his brain. So I talk to my friend, she has daughter who work with autistic people. My friend tell me autistic kids, they really not speak nothing, they make sounds only. But my son, he can talk."

Clearly, this mother needed information, and just as clearly the information needed to be presented in such a way that it could be useful to her. An administrator striving to provide high-quality preschool inclusive services that are family centered must consider not only the specific information needs of families, but also how the families will access the information. In the next section we discuss both of these considerations.

Providing Parents With Information About Disabilities

When parents learn they have a child with disabilities, they usually want as much information as they can possibly get about the disability. Early childhood professionals, however, should understand that the family's need-to-know may be more pressing than making placement decisions or learning about the IEP. When parents first learn their child has disabilities, the information they most likely want includes:

- **How the disability affects their child's development**

- **What to expect for the child's future (both short term future of elementary school and the long-term expectations when the school years are over)**

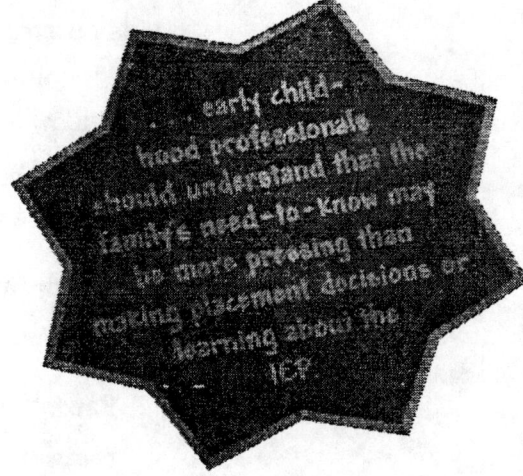

early childhood professionals should understand that the family's need-to-know may be more pressing than making placement decisions or learning about the IEP.

Chapter Seven

- **What, if any, medications are appropriate**

- **If the disability is inherited**

After parents have learned about the nature of their child's disability, they begin needing information about the service system and their child's educational programs. If the parents learned about the child's disability during the child's first three years of life, the state early intervention system may have provided some of this information. Nevertheless, we encourage early childhood personnel working with families to begin the conversation about services by finding out what type of information the parents need.

Providing Parents With Information About the Special Education Process

Most family members are not educators. When a child is referred for special education services, the family may have little understanding of the assessment-placement-IEP process. Furthermore, they may know nothing about their rights as parents. Thus, one of the first things an early childhood educator should do with parents new to the special education process, is assess the family's understanding and need for information.

Providing Parents With Information About Their Rights

While some administrators may feel the family is responsible for learning about their rights, other administrators feel ethically responsible to provide parents with information about their (and their child's) rights. It is our position that families whose children are entering the system should, at a minimum, have the following information:

- **Children with disabilities have the right to a free appropriate public education**

- **Children with disabilities should be educated in the least restrictive environment**

- **Parents who suspect their child has an impairment may request an evaluation**

- Parents should understand and agree (in writing) to any evaluation and placement decisions

- Children should be tested in the language they understand best

- Parents must be notified in writing if the school proposes to make changes in a child's program, conduct an evaluation, or refuse a request for an evaluation

- Parents can request a re-evaluation of their child

- Parents have the right to review their child's records and to have any errors corrected

- Parents should participate in the development of their child's IEP

- Parents should be kept informed about their child's progress

- Parents can request mediation or due process if differences are not satisfactorily resolved at the school level

Providing Parents With Information About the IEP Meeting

In addition to understanding their rights under the law, parents should know about the process by which a placement decision is made for their child. Ensuring the initial meeting with parents and the IEP/placement meeting are family-centered is an important part of inclusive preschool services for families and children. Parents should be informed ahead of time about what to expect in their child's IEP meeting and they should know what will be expected of them. Administrators should ensure that parents receive information from professionals in a jargon-free and sensitive manner. When parents know what is going on, they are less likely to be intimidated by the process and, thus, more likely to participate productively in the meeting. One very articulate mother expressed to us her feeling about the placement process.

> "They just don't make the process accessible. The terminology used in an ARD meeting will blow your mind. You're intimidated, you've got a psychologist there. They don't even speak a language that's non-lawyer or non-special ed. friendly. They make parents feel like they can't ask questions. And the parents don't want to feel stupid so they don't ask questions until after the assessments are gone over."

Providing Parents With Information About Options

As we noted in the Family Summary Point #3, parents often feel that there are few service options for their child and they have limited participation in making a choice about their child's placement. Not only do administrators need to ensure that a range of choices exist in the system, they must make sure family members are made aware of the options and have a voice in the placement decision. Two examples from the ECRII study illustrate these concerns. A school administrator, when asked if parents of young children with disabilities were told that Head Start is a inclusive option, said:

> "Well, as a general rule, we don't tell all parents about that [Head Start is an inclusive option]. In some situations we might suggest it to a parent, but we don't tell every parent because it is an income eligibility type of thing."

And, a mother conveyed frustration with the IEP meeting in the following comment:

> "I guess the down and out of it is that I didn't have a choice. Well, I did have a choice—he either goes [to a nonintegrated class] or he doesn't. That was the choice and it wasn't acceptable—having him not go." (Beckman et al., in press)

Providing Parents With Information About Program Quality

Another issue about which administrators should be aware is parent's perspective of program quality. In some systems, if the placement decision is a community-based setting, the parents are allowed to choose the child care center their child will attend. Although the parents may be offered a range of programs from which to choose, the quality of all programs is likely to vary and there is potential for parents to select a program in which the quality of the early childhood education is poor. Parents should have information about quality indicators in early childhood programs so they can make informed choices about their child's placement. In Chapter 3, we described the characteristics of high quality early childhood programs and provide a checklist for evaluating program quality. This information could be useful for some parents.

Parents also should understand that quality of inclusive preschools is reflected in the individual experiences planned for their child. As we noted in Chapter 3, we believe that children with disabilities benefit from their experiences in a high quality early childhood environment and their interactions with typically developing peers. But, specialized instruction must occur in those

high quality early childhood environments. Often, however, specialized instruction occurs in the form of naturalistic instruction, and may look quite different from the traditional ideas many parents have about teaching (i.e., where the teacher leads the class in didactic instruction, such as reading or math lessons). Therefore, what a parent may see as baby-sitting in a child care center (e.g., their child participating independently in a center time activity) actually may be a planned and important individualized learning opportunity. It is important that parents have information about the inclusion process and information about naturalistic teaching strategies. Investigators with the ECRII have developed a series of parent materials called *Me Too!* (Hanson & Beckman, in press) that provides information about what to look for when observing inclusive programs. Information about these materials appears at the end of this chapter.

Administrators also should ensure that families are never put in situations where they must choose between inclusive programs that do not provide for the special needs of their child or segregated programs that offer specialized services. One of our ECRII synthesis points stated that programs must be ready for children rather than requiring children to be ready for programs. This means that the services in the inclusive program should be as intense as the services in a segregated special education classrooms. Conveying this belief to parents, and substantiating it by providing the necessary support for individual children in inclusive settings is essential for administrators who work with families.

Providing Parents With Information About Parental Responsibilities

Not only do parents need information about the special education process and their rights under IDEA, they also must understand their responsibilities. Much has been written about the need to empower families to take an active role in their child's special education program. In an at-

tempt to advocate for their child, however, family members may appear confrontational, which might alienate special education administrators and staff. In the booklet, *My Community, My Family* (part of the *Me Too!* series), information is provided to families and school personnel about ways to build good working relationships with the school. Specifically, good relationships are built on:

Positive attitudes :

- · Starting with a clean slate
- · Being nonjudgmental
- · Noticing the good things in others

Mutual respect for :

- · Beliefs and cultural traditions
- · Others' knowledge
- · Priorities and values
- · Time and resources

Trust :

- · Follow-through on promises and commitments
- · Honesty
- · Confidentiality

Communication :

- · Regular and causal
- · Includes positive comments, not just complaints

Providing Parents With Information About Parenting a Child With Disabilities

Parents often want information about how to teach their child or how to manage their child's behavior. Because the home environment is vital to a child's development, it is critically important that parents of young children with disabilities obtain the parenting information they need. Again, we refer you to the *Me Too!* series, which provides parents with practical suggestions they may use at home or in the community. A range of other informational resources for families also is available. At the end of the chapter we provide suggestions for obtaining further information.

Providing Support to Families

Support to families comes in many forms. The simplest and most obvious form of support is a positive and welcoming attitude. When teachers and school staff interact positively with a child with disabilities, the child's parents naturally feel supported. Likewise when their information needs are met, parents typically feel supported. But, parents of children with disabilities have many additional stresses, and they often need more than a daily dose of casual support offered by a positive staff member. Many avenues exist for a family-centered preschool programs to provide family support. Below, we list some suggestions:

- **Bring families together to provide support and expertise to each other**

- **Encourage parents to visit and participate in school activities**

- **Plan special events and invite parents**

- **Keep families informed about ongoing activities (newsletter's are great)**

- Provide families with names and contact information related to community agencies that also offer support to families of children with disabilities

- Ensure families are not excluded from participation in the school programs because of transportation difficulties

- Hold meetings at times convenient to the family

- Recognize the perspective family members bring to the team and value their insight

- Have procedures for conflict resolution

Some early childhood programs, such as Head Start, have an active family component. Other programs, however, provide little support to parents of children with disabilities. Having an organized mechanism to provide support to families of young children with disabilities will certainly be another administrative challenge. Keep in mind, however, parents know best what their children need. When family needs are supported and their energies harnessed, a potentially powerful partnership can be forged. Parents can assist you in breaking down barriers to providing high quality inclusive preschool services. Very often parent voices can be persuasive (for example at school board meetings or in the superintendents' offices) when your voice is completely ignored. Drawing parents into your program through supportive activities is a way to meet their needs and at the same time build a foundation of support for your own program.

often parent voices can be persuasive (for example at school board meetings or in the superintendents' offices) when your voice is completely ignored.

Chapter Seven

Resources for Working with Families

Books and Articles

Beckman, P. J. (1996). *Strategies for working with families of young children with disabilities.* Baltimore:Paul H. Brookes Publishing Co.

Dunst, C., Trivett, C., & Deal, A. (1988). *Enabling and empowering families: Principles and guidelines for practice.* Cambridge, MA: Brookline Books.

Lynch, E. W., & Hanson, M. J. (Eds.). (1998). *Developing cross cultural competence: A guide for working with young children and their families,* 2nd Ed. Baltimore: Paul H. Brookes Publishing Co.

Singer, G. H. S. & Powers, L. E. (1993). *Families, disability, and empowerment: Active coping skills and strategies for family interventions.* Baltimore: Paul H. Brookes Publishing Co.

Informational Materials

Hanson, M. J. & Beckman, P. J. (in press). *Me Too!* Baltimore: Paul H. Brookes Publishing Co.

> Booklets included in the *Me Too!* series:
> Introducing... Me!
> It's Time for Preschool
> My Community, My Family
> Me and My New Friends
> On My Best Behavior
> Look What I Can Do Now

McWilliam, P. J., & Winton, P. (1992). *Brass tacks: Part I—Programs and practices; Part II—Individual interactions with families.* Chapel Hill, NC: Frank Porter Graham Publications Office.

National Information Center on Children and Youth with Disabilities (NICHCY) Washington, DC. Offers a variety of information and resources for parents (see internet address below).

Internet Resources

Early Childhood Research Institute on Culturally and Linguistically Appropriate Services. University of Illinois at Urbana-Champaign. www.clas.uiuc.edu/abtclas

National Information Center on Children and Youth with Disabilities (NICHCY) www.nichcy.org/pubs/parents

The Family Village - bringing together valuable information for parents of individuals who have disabilities. www.familyvillage.wisc.edu

Chapter Eight

Systems Change

Systems Change: Moving to Inclusion

Through our ECRII research of supports and barriers to preschool inclusion, we have identified several influences that impact the success (or failure) of building and maintaining inclusive programs. In the earlier chapters of this guide, we presented information to help administrators support and improve the inclusive services that currently exist. In this chapter we discuss issues related to *systems change*, specifically, changing non-inclusive programs into inclusive programs. We begin by restating one of the ECRII synthesis points: *Programs, not children, have to be ready for inclusion.* We believe a philosophy of program readiness provides a framework for building high quality programs that provide high quality inclusive services.

The press for inclusion comes from a variety of forces. Often this force is the result of legislative mandates, as expressed in the following comment:

> "We have been instructed by our legal department that we must very carefully look at the least restrictive options for the children and be able to justify why we cannot provide services to them in less restrictive placements." - Preschool coordinator

Other forces behind systems change efforts include parents of children who participated in inclusive programs as infants and toddlers, pressure from the advocacy community, the national trends toward inclusion, and even the perception of financial or logical incentives.

Chapter Eight

Whatever the reason for initiating an inclusion change effort, the systemic contexts within which the changes will occur can vary considerably. Because of these contextual differences, we realize a definitive plan for bringing about systems change in every context is unlikely to be useful. Thus, in this chapter, we present and discuss some of the logistical concerns that influence change efforts. We frame our discussion around the following five categories of influence that emerged from our research (Lieber, et al., in press):

- **Key Individuals**

- **Shared Vision**

- **Organizational Structure**

- **Policy Impact**

- **External Support and Community Influences**

Within each of these categories, we provide some guidelines to assist an administrator who might be in a position to influence or lead an effort to change a non-inclusive service system into an inclusive system. We believe these key influence principles may be helpful to anyone embarking on efforts to initiate new inclusive services. At the end of the chapter we provide a list of resources that provide more detailed information on system change efforts.

Inclusion Influence #1: Key Individuals

Critical to any change effort is the commitment of individuals in leadership roles who recognize the need for change and also the importance of consensus building. In addition to playing an important role in the logistics of any change effort, key individuals can set the tone among staff that all children with disabilities should have access to inclusive preschool classes as their first option.

Systems Change

An administrator faced with the challenges of beginning inclusive pre-school services must recruit those key individuals who are in positions to influence the system's change process. Although many individuals might participate in the change effort, we discuss below three constituent groups that should be represented on the systems change team.

System-Level Individuals

Many decisions around change for preschool inclusion will depend on the organizational structure of the system you want to change. Thus, it is important to include individuals from within the systems who understand the various program configuration possibilities and the challenges presented by each possibility. These individuals may be superintendents or their assistants, directors of special services, or early childhood coordinators.

Program Director

When inclusion occurs in a community-based program or Head Start program, primary influence in the success or failure of any preschool inclusion effort is advocacy voiced by a program director. The leadership of a program director who is visibly involved in the inclusion efforts will prove invaluable. A proactive and committed program director will provide the necessary support and staff development, will set the tone for collaboration, and will strive to provide high quality inclusive services.

Parents

Because parents are primary stakeholders in the inclusive program, they need to be part of the process when plans are made for starting preschool services and also after the services are started. Parent input can be important and should be appreciated. We discuss parent involvement in detail in Chapter 7.

Chapter Eight

Inclusion Influence #2: Shared Vision

Linked closely with the influence of key individuals is the influence of a shared vision for inclusion. Although there are many forms of inclusion, an important component of the change effort is that the key individuals share a similar vision of preschool inclusion and its mission. For over two decades, advocates have argued that individuals with disabilities have the value-based right to inclusion. Using these arguments, others have identified some specific values that support inclusion. Bailey, McWilliam, Buysse, and Wesley (1998) have suggested three inclusion values that we believe should be the basis of any systems change team's shared vision for inclusion. These inclusion values are:

- **All children should be in programs/settings of high quality**

- **Services should address the special learning needs of children with disabilities**

- **Services should be family-centered**

Although having a shared value-based vision is important, and can guide your planning and decision making, such vision alone is NOT sufficient for ensuring a successful system change effort. As an administrator, you know very well that any change effort requires a lot of hard work. As with any effective intervention, systems change efforts require careful planning, implementation, and evaluation. Before we outline some planning considerations, however, we offer an often heard caveat: *"Proceed carefully and plan thoroughly."*

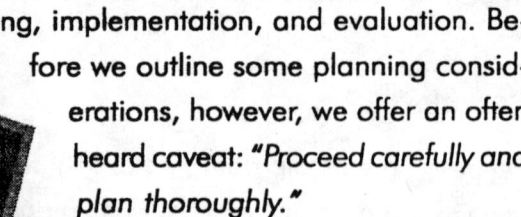

 Systems Change

"We needed to get people out of their boxes. Our early childhood programs were operating independently, not paying attention to each other, doing their own thing . . . We wanted a mission or vision for the entire system instead of a mission or vision for each program. We first tried to deal with the separate programs, hoping they would all see the vision. But, that didn't work. So we reorganized with an effort to break down some of the barriers so everyone would see the greater vision – not just their own program."
- School System Administrator

Getting Started

Develop a program philosophy

In Chapter 5 we shared a program philosophy developed by the Experimental Education Unit, an inclusive preschool program at the University of Washington. Although the philosophy statement your team adopts may be somewhat different, we encourage you to use the inclusion values presented in Table 1 as a basis for your philosophy.

Define program goals

In addition to a program philosophy, the team needs to identify broad goals for the inclusive program being initiated. Following are Bailey and Wolery's (1992) seven goals of early intervention. Not only can these goals be used to guide your system change planning efforts, they also can provide a context for developing your program philosophy.

Chapter Eight

- Support families in achieving their own goals

- Promote children's engagement, independence, and mastery

- Promote children's development in key domains

- Build and support children's social competence

- Promote children's generalized use of skills

- Provide and prepare children for normalized life experiences

- Prevent the emergence of future problems or disabilities

Define roles, responsibilities, and timelines

Delineating the roles, responsibilities, and timelines is a major task of the systems change team. An understanding of "who does what and when" will ease the transition to inclusive services. During our ECRII study, a school system with which we were working was going through a system change effort. We share some highlights of that system change effort to illustrate how roles, responsibilities, and time lines play-out in a real situation. The process began with a new administrator who had a broad inclusion vision. This individual recruited a few individuals to form a strategic planning team. The team adopted an inclusion philosophy, established inclusion goals, and decided to begin their inclusion effort the following school year. Next, the team established a Preschool Task Force that included representataives from the school system, the community, and a local university. During the initial Task Force meetings the group generated a list of immediate and long-term concerns. Based on these concerns, sub-committees were formed and roles, responsibilities, and time lines were established. Over the next several months, the committees identified existing problems within the system, reviewed inclusion models in comparable systems, and formalized specific recommendations for change.

The process was arduous and at times overwhelming. Problems did occur, and at times emotions were tense. Nevertheless, at the beginning of the following school year changes were in place to pilot a community-based inclusion program. This pilot program, jointly with the work of the Task Force, led to a system-wide adoption of inclusion as the primary mode of service delivery.

Plan the scope of the inclusion effort

Decisions about the full scope of the inclusion effort should be made during the planning stages. Does the team want to go for a full-inclusion effort in which children with and without disabilities attend the same program for the same amount of time each day? Will the inclusion preschool program be one of several options for services or will it be the primary option available to children? We recommend that decisions about services always be based on the child's needs and families' priorities, but when planning services, we also recommend that inclusive preschool services are the first option considered.

Plan how disability awareness of regular early childhood staff will be delivered

We are sure you know that many early childhood educators have limited knowledge and understanding of disabilities. Preservice, inservice, and ongoing support must be planned and provided to the early childhood staff who will be involved in the inclusion change. Because we devote an entire chapter to inservice and staff development, (see Chapter 5) we do not discuss disability awareness in this section.

Be Aware of Attitudinal Barriers and Resistance Issues

In addition to the logistical concerns, the systems change team should be aware of attitudinal barriers or resistance issues that are likely to surface. In a nationwide survey of barriers to preschool inclusion, Smith and Rose (1993) identified the following five categories of attitudinal barriers.

- **Turf Barriers**
- **Teacher Preparedness Barriers**
- **Disability Awareness Barriers**
- **Communication, Collaboration, & Respect Barriers**
- **"Someone Will Lose" Barriers**

So that your systems change team is prepared to address some of the resistance that may occur in both the planning and implementation stages of your change effort, we briefly discuss these barriers.

Turf Attitudes

This barrier relates to the perception that early childhood special educators think their early childhood colleagues, *"Don't even try to work with our children."* And, concerns that the early childhood educators think, *"I'm expected to be the special education teacher and work with their children."*

Teacher Preparedness Attitudes

This barrier relates to common beliefs about training. Because early childhood educators are not specifically trained to work with children with disabilities, many believe they should not have children with disabilities placed in their classrooms.

Awareness Attitudes

A clearly identified attitudinal barrier found in Smith and Rose's survey was the lack of knowledge around disability awareness. When individuals do not understand the educational, medical, and physical needs of children with specific disabilities, fears and misinformation about inclusion can exist.

Communication/Collaboration/Respect Attitudes

Survey respondents also reported a lack of communication and information sharing between and among professionals, programs, and families. This void results in misinformation and lack of respect. Our ECRII research has also found lack of communication as a major barrier.

"Someone Will Lose" Attitude

This barrier relates to beliefs that children do not benefit from inclusion. The general attitude expressed by survey participants was that both children with disabilities and children without disabilities are more likely to receive fewer and less services in inclusive programs than they would receive in segregated programs.

Chapter Eight

Inclusion Influence #3: Organizational Structure

A third key influence of successful inclusion is organizational structure. In Chapter 2 of this Guide, we describe three organizational structures identified in our ECRII research, and we discuss some challenges presented by each of those models. We do not repeat that discussion, however, we highlight some features of those organizational contexts that you may want to consider in your system change planning.

Community-Based Child Care

Often, the primary reasons for choosing a community-based preschool programs to begin an inclusion effort is location and the relationship the family of a child with disabilities has with the program. Location and family relationships, however, are not the only important selection criteria. Your systems change team will have to consider issues such as program quality, tuition complications, and transportation. In addition, because teachers in community-based programs are generally not employed by the school system, it may be more difficult to establish individualized programs for meeting the special needs of a child with disabilities than in programs where the teachers are school employees.

Head Start Programs

Inclusive options for preschool children with disabilities are sometimes available in Head Start programs. National policy mandates that Head Start serve children with disabilities, however, most children with disabilities being served in Head Start have mild disabilities. There is a move to provide Head Start services to children with more severe disabilities, and this may create opportunities for public school districts and Head Start programs to jointly establish inclusive options for children with disabilities.

If you are considering Head Start as an inclusive option for children with disabilities, there are several administrative challenges you need to consider. For example, who develops a child's IEP, and who implements it? If IEPs are developed by the school district and related services are provided by the school district, the Head Start teachers must have opportunity to consult or collaborate with the school district personnel. Philosophical differences also must be considered. Head Start teachers may follow a "strict" developmentally appropriate practice belief which may run counter to the early childhood special education belief in specialized teaching strategies. Even though these beliefs systems are often much more alike than different, the perception of different philosophies cannot be ignored.

Public School Classes

It is becoming increasingly common for public school systems to provide preschool programs for typically developing children. Clearly, it is much easier to initiate an inclusive effort in an existing public school preschool program than to initiate an inclusive program where no preschool options for typically developing children exist. Logistical problems, such as tuition, transportation, and different regulations are avoided in the public school context. Teachers employed by the school system typically have certification and school administrators have more control over quality indicators such as class size, teacher:child ratio, curriculum, materials, and equipment.

Nevertheless, there are some challenges to providing inclusive services in existing public school programs. If special education services are delivered by itinerant specialists, collaboration between classroom and itinerant staff is critically important. Likewise, coordination and collaboration must occur if different administrative units exist within the same system. Often, roles and responsibilities need to be redefined.

Chapter Eight

Inclusion Influence #4: Policy Impact

ECRII researchers found that policies can both facilitate inclusion efforts and impede such efforts. Nevertheless, policies certainly dictate the direction of your efforts, and early intervention research indicates there is a lot of policy misinformation. In their national survey of policy issues, Smith and Rose (1993) identified categories of policies that influence inclusion. Despite differences in various state and local policies, the issues and concerns were remarkably similar. A policy issue that significantly impacts one system change effort, might have little or no impact on another effort, yet every change effort will likely face some policy impact. To provide you with some ideas for dealing with the policy impact, we briefly discuss some of Smith and Rose's policy categories.

Personnel Standard Policies

In some states, policy requires that individuals in special education positions meet specified state standards. A misinterpretation of this policy can lead to the notion that a community-based preschool cannot become inclusive unless an early childhood special education teacher is hired. Considering various options, however, could prevent such a policy misinterpretation from becoming a barrier to inclusion. For example, Smith and Rose report that some states ensured special education services were provided under the *supervision* of a certified special educator, and other states avoided the perceived barrier by providing *itinerant* services.

Fiscal Policies

Policies that relate to allocation of funds frequently present concerns. Funding formulas and funds allocated for specific groups of children often become barriers to inclusion. Although options typically are situational, careful policy analysis and interpretations can sometimes lead to the elimination of perceived barriers. For example, we found an administrator who successfully mixed children with different funding streams and simply docu-

mented the services provided to all children. Likewise, Smith and Rose report that young children with IEPs were placed in community-based programs and funds were paid for the amount of time required to implement the IEP. Exploring the options to reduce or eliminate the impact of fiscal policy barriers may require considerable effort from your change team. Nevertheless, we think you would agree, time spent reducing fiscal barriers is time well spent!

Eligibility Policies

Numerous policies relate to criteria for determining who is eligible to receive various educational services. Some of these, such as Head Start policies, are defined at a national level, while others are defined at a program level. Options to barriers posed by eligibility policy at the national level may be limited, although we know some administrators have found satisfactory solutions. For example, working cooperatively, some Head Starts and LEAs have combined programs while keeping the administrative structure separate. Certainly, an option like this is not ideal, but it creatively facilitates an inclusion effort. If eligibility policy barriers are defined at the program level, a plan to develop new policy may be the most obvious and also the easiest option.

Transportation Policies

You know, better than we, the complexities of transportation policies. A major policy impact related to transportation is scheduling. If transportation policies are not flexible, it may be impossible to arrange transportation for some children. An option many programs use is to reimburse families who provide their child's transportation. Other administrators have arranged a service exchange plan whereby one agency provides transportation in exchange for another service provided by the other agency. Yet another option that has been successful in some situations, is to define transportation as a necessary related service for implementing a child's program, thus making it a required service.

Chapter Eight

We believe it is very important to recognize that policy misinterpretation is often a major barrier to successful change efforts. Smith and Rose caution us to never assume we know what a policy means. Because misinterpretations often have been passed down through the "generations," they recommend obtaining a copy of the policy and conducting your own policy analysis. Then, if you are still unsure, request clarification—"but never assume there is a policy barrier."

Inclusion Influence #5:
External Support and Community Influences

The final key influence of successful inclusion efforts is the type and amount of external support. Although external financial support is obviously a factor in any successful change effort, we found many other external and community influences. Sometimes, however, an external influence operates as a facilitator to successful inclusion efforts, yet in other situations they operate as barriers. We discuss briefly some specific external influences you might incorporate into your inclusion effort.

Influence of higher education

We found that early childhood special education teacher training programs can play an important role in inclusion efforts. When teacher training programs need inclusion sites for practice teaching placements, their influence in the community can be powerful. One way in which a local teacher training program might facilitate your inclusion effort is to enter into a partnership whereby you provide access to placement sites in exchange for inservice and workshop training. Another way in which institutions of higher education might facilitate inclusion efforts is through research projects. Administrators in the programs where ECRII research was conducted indicated to us that their programs benefited considerably from being part of a university directed research project.

Influence of other programs

We found the old adage "Seeing is believing" to be a powerful facilitator of inclusion. When teachers were provided an opportunity to visit a "model" program and see for themselves how inclusion could work, they were more eager to return to their own classrooms and implement changes. Likewise, staff in the model programs were proud of being recognized and were encouraged to continue providing high quality inclusive services.

Influence from within the system

Sometimes within a system, influences come in the form of incentives, training, and special recognition. We also found that systems were sometimes willing to implement pilot programs as a means of reducing risks. And, successful pilot programs are likely to become successful established programs!

Influence of community advocacy

Most certainly, families are a loud voice in community advocacy, but many community agencies also play an important role for initiating inclusion. As you develop your plan for inclusion, it will be important to enlist the support of these various agencies. In addition, joint planning and collaboration with existing community supports should be considered. For example, one inclusive preschool program in our research was housed in a high school. High school students were recruited to serve as tutors, and, as you might expect, former tutors were enrolling their own children in the preschool program!

Summary

As we noted at the beginning of this chapter, states are different, communities are different, and situations are different. Thus, a one-size-fits-all, action plan for initiating inclusion cannot be described. In our investigations of how inclusion programs were initiated and how they were maintained over time, we identified key influences that facilitated successful inclusion. We also found, however, that sometimes the key influences were not facilitators of successful inclusion at all, but rather served as facilitators of failed inclusion efforts (or barriers to success, as we more politely refer to them). Nevertheless, we optimistically see the glass as "half-full"!

As you embark on efforts to bring about inclusion, we encourage you to consider the larger picture of inclusion in your state and community, but to focus your efforts on the small picture. That is, work carefully to bring about change to your local situation. We believe the key influences that facilitated inclusion efforts in the programs we studied are the same key influences you will need to consider in planning and implementing your system change efforts.

Recommended Readings

Smith, B. J., & Rose, D. F. (1993). *Administrator's policy handbook for preschool mainstreaming.* Cambridge, MA: Brookline Books.

Strain, P. S., Smith, B. J., & McWilliam, R. A. (1996). The widespread adoption of service delivery recommendations: A systems change perspective. In S. L. Odom & M. E. McLean (Eds.). *Early intervention/early childhood special education: Recommended practices* (pp. 101-124). Austin, TX: Pro Ed.

References

An Administrator's Guide

Bailey, D. B., McWilliam, R. A., Buysse, V. & Wesley, P. A. (1998). Inclusion in the context of competing values in early childhood education. *Early Childhood Research Quarterly, 13,* 27-49.

Bailey, D. B. & Wolery, M. (1992). *Teaching infants and preschoolers with disabilities.* 2nd ed. Columbus OH: Merrill Publishing Co.

Beckman, P. J., Greig, D., Barnwell, D., Hanson, M. J., Horn, E., & Sandall, S. R. (in press). Influences on family perceptions of inclusive preschool programs. *Journal of Early Intervention.*

Bredekamp, S., & Copple, C. (1997). *Developmentally appropriate practice in early childhood programs, Revised edition.* Washington, DC: National Association for the Education of Young Children.

Bruder, M. B. (1994). Working with members of other disciplines: Collaboration for success. In M. Wolery & J. S. Wilbers (Eds.), *Including children with special needs in early childhood programs* (pp. 45 – 70). Washington, DC: National Association for the Education of Young Children.

Bruder, M. B. (1998). A collaborative model to increase the capacity of childcare providers to include young children with disabilities. *Journal of Early Intervention, 21,* 177-186.

Hanson, M. J., & Beckman, P. J. (Eds.) (in press) *Me Too!* Baltimore: Brookes Publishing Co.

Hanson, M. J., Beckman, P. J., Horn, E., Marquart, J., Sandall, S. R., Grieg, D., Brennan, E. (in press). Entering preschool: Family and professional experiences in this transition process. *Journal of Early Intervention.*

Hanson, M. J., Wolfberg, P., Zercher, C., Morgan, M., Guiterrez, S., Barnwell, D., & Beckman, P. (1998). The culture of inclusion: Recognizing diversity at multiple levels. *Early Childhood Research Quarterly, 13,* 185-211.

Hargreaves. A. (1997). *Rethinking educational change with heart and mind.* Alexandria, VA: Association for Supervision and Curriculum Development.

Harms, T., Clifford, R. M., & Cryer, D. (1998). *Early Childhood Environment Rating Scale—Revised* (ECERS-R).New York: Teachers College Press.

Hyson, M. C., Hirsch–Pasek, K., & Rescorla, L. (1990). The classroom practices inventory: An observation instrument based on the NAEYC's guidelines for developmentally appropriate practices for 4- and 5-year-old children. *Early Childhood Research Quarterly, 5,* 475-494.

Jones, H. A., & Rapport, M. J. (1997). Research to practice in inclusive early childhood education. *Teaching Exceptional Children, 29(2),* 57-61.

Lieber, J., Hanson, M. J, Beckman, P. J., Odom, S. L., Sandall, S. R., Horn, E., & Wolery, R. A. (in press). Key influences on the initiation and implementation of inclusive preschool programs. *Exceptional Children.*

McWilliam, R. A. (1996). How to provide integrated therapy. In R. A. McWilliam (Ed.), *Rethinking pull-out services in early intervention: A professional resource* (pp. 147 – 184). Baltimore: Paul Brookes Publishing Co.

National Information Center on Children and Youth with Disabilities (NICHCY) www.nichcy.org

ECRII Administrator's Guide

Odom S. L., Hanson, M. J., Lieber, J., Marquart, J., Sandall, S., Wolery, R. A., Horn, E., Schwartz, I., Beckman, P. J., Hikido, C., & Chambers, J. (2000). *The costs of preschool inclusion.* Manuscript submitted for publication.

Odom, S. L., Horn, E. M., Marquart, J., Hanson, M. J., Wolfberg, P., Beckman, P., Lieber, J., Li, S., Schwartz, I., Janko, S., & Sandall, S. (1999). On the forms of inclusion: Organizational context and service delivery models. *Journal of Early Intervention, 22,* 185-199.

Quality Indicators: Early Childhood Special Education. (1996). Seattle: University of Washington, Experimental Education Unit.

Raab, M. M. & Dunst, C. J. (1997).*The Preschool Assessment of the Classroom Environment Scale—Revised* (PACE-R). Asheville, NC: Orelena Hawks Puckett Institute; 189 E. Chestnut St.

Sandall, S., Schwartz, I., Joseph, G., Chou, H. Y., Horn, E., Libber, J., Odom, S., Wolery, R. A., and the ECRII (in press). *Building Blocks for successful early childhood programs: Strategies for including all children.* Baltimore: Brookes Publishing Co.

Sexton, D., Snyder, P., Wolfe, B. Lobman, M., Stricklin, S., & Akers, P. (1996). Early intervention inservice training strategies: Perceptions and suggestions from the field. *Exceptional Children, 62,* 486-495.

Skinner, D., Rodriguez, P., & Bailey, D. B. (1999). Qualitative analyses of Latino parents' religious interpretations of their child's disability. *Journal of Early Intervention, 22,* 271-285.

Smith, B. J., & Rose, D. F. (1993). *Administrator's policy handbook for preschool mainstreaming.* Cambridge, MA: Brookline Books.

ECRII Administrators' Guide

Trohanis, P. L. (1994). Planning for successful inservice education for local early childhood programs. *Topics in Early Childhood Special Education, 14,* 311-332.

Vaughn, S., Schumm, J. S., & Arguelles, J. E. (1997). The ABCDEs of co-teaching. *Teaching Exceptional Children, 30,* 4–10.

Verduin, J., Miller, H., & Greer, C. (1977). *Adults teaching adults.* Austin, TX: Learning Concepts.

Wolery, M., Paucca, T., Brashers, M. S., & Grant, S. (2000). *Quality of Inclusive Experiences Measure.* Chapel Hill: University of North Carolina, FPG Child Development Center.

Glossary

An Administrator's Guide

From the National Information Center on Children and Youth with Disabilities (NICHCY) Washington, DC

Assessment – (1) collecting and bringing together information about a child's needs; may include social, psychological, and educational evaluations used to determine services. (2) a process using observation, testing, and test analysis to determine an individual's strengths and weaknesses in order to plan his or her educational services

Assessment team - a team of people from different backgrounds who observe and test a child to determine his or her strengths and weaknesses

At risk - a term used with children who have, or could have, problems with their development that may affect later learning

Child Find - a service directed by each state's Department of Education or lead agency for identifying and diagnosing unserved children with disabilities; while Child Find looks for all unserved children, it makes a special effort to identify children from birth to six years old

Comprehensive service system - refers to a list of 14 areas each participating state is to provide under early intervention services. These 14 points range from definition of developmentally delayed, to guidelines for identification, assessment, and provision of early intervention services for the child and family, and include timelines and quality control

Developmental history - the developmental progress of a child (ages birth to 18 years) in such skills as sitting, walking, talking, or learning

Glossary

Developmental tests - standardized tests that measure a child's development as it compares to the development of all other children at that age

Disability - the result of any physical or mental condition that affects or prevents one's ability to develop, achieve, and/or function in an educational setting at a normal rate

Due process (procedure) - action that protects a person's rights; in special education, this applies to action taken to protect the educational rights of students with disabilities

Early intervention services or programs - programs or services designed to identify and treat a developmental problem as early as possible, before age 3 (services for 3-5 year olds are referred to as preschool services)

Eligible - able to qualify

Evaluation - (as applied to children from birth through two years of age) the procedures used to determine if a child is eligible for early intervention services; (as applied to preschool and school-aged children) the procedures used to determine whether a child has a disability and the nature and extent of the special education and related services the child needs

Free appropriate public education [often referred to as FAPE] - one of the key requirements of IDEA, which requires that an education program be provided for all school-aged children (regardless of disability) without cost to families; the exact requirements of "appropriate" are not defined, but other references within the law imply the most "normal" setting available

Handicap - see disability

Identification - the process of locating and identifying children needing special services

Individualized Education Program (IEP) - a written education plan for a school-aged child with disabilities developed by a team of professionals (teachers, therapists, etc.) and the child's parents; it is reviewed and updated yearly and describes how the child is presently doing, what the child's learning needs are, and what services the child will need; (For children ages birth through 2 years, the IFSP is used.)

Individualized Family Service Plan (IFSP) - a written statement for an infant or toddler (ages birth through 2 years old) developed by a team of people who have worked with the child and the family; the IFSP must describe the child's development levels; family information; major outcomes expected to be achieved for the child and family; the services the child will be receiving; when and where the child will receive these services; and the steps to be taken to support the transition of the child to another program; the IFSP will also list the name of the service coordinator assigned to the child and his/her family

Individuals with Disabilities Education Act (IDEA) – see Public Law (P.L.) 94-142

Lead agency - the agency (office) within a state or territory in charge of overseeing and coordinating service systems for children ages birth through two

Least Restrictive Environment (LRE) - an educational setting or program that provides a student with disabilities with the chance to work and learn to the best of his or her ability; it also provides the student as much contact as possible with children without disabilities, while meeting all of the child's learning needs and physical requirements

Multidisciplinary - a team approach involving specialists in more than one discipline, such as a team made up of a physical therapist, a speech and language pathologist, a child development specialist, an occupational therapist, or other specialists as needed

Glossary

Occupational therapy   - a therapy or treatment provided by an occupational therapist that helps individual developmental or physical skills that will aid in daily living; it focuses on sensory integration, on coordination of movement, and on fine motor and self-help skills, such as dressing, eating with a fork and spoon, etc.

Parent training and information programs   - programs that provide information to parents of children with special needs about acquiring services, working with schools and educators to ensure the most effective educational placement for their child, understanding the methods of testing and evaluating a child with special needs, and making informed decisions about their child's special needs

Physical therapy   - treatment of (physical) disabilities given by a trained physical therapist (under doctor's orders) that includes the use of massage, exercise, etc. to help the person improve the use of bones, muscles, joints, and nerves

Placement   - the classroom, program, service, and/or therapy that is selected for a student with special needs

Policy/policies   - rules and regulations; as related to early intervention and special education programs, the rules that a state or local school system has for providing services for and educating its students with special needs

Private agency   - a non-public agency which may be receiving public funds to provide services for some children

Private therapist   - any professional (therapist, tutor, psychologist, etc.) not connected with the public school system or with a public agency

Program(s)   - in special education, a service, placement, and/or therapy designed to help a child with special needs

Psychologist   - a specialist in the field of psychology, usually having a Master's degree or Ph.D. in psychology

Public agency   - an agency, office, or organization that is supported by public funds and serves the community at large

Public Law (P.L.) 94-142   - a law passed in 1975 requiring that public schools provide a "free appropriate public education" to school-aged children ages 3-21 (exact ages depend on your state's mandate), regardless of disabling condition; also called the Education For All Handicapped Children Act, with recent amendments (P. L. 99-457) now called the Individuals with Disabilities Education Act (IDEA)

Public Law (P.L.) 102-119   - passed in 1991, this is an amendment to the Individuals with Disabilities Education Act (IDEA), which requires states and territories to provide a "free appropriate public education" to all children ages 3-21; and provides funds for states and territories to plan a comprehensive service system for infants and toddlers (ages birth through 2 years) with disabilities related services - transportation and developmental, corrective, and other support services that a child with disabilities requires in order to benefit from education; examples of related services include: speech pathology and audiology, psychological services, physical and occupational therapy, recreation, counseling services, interpreters for the hearing impaired, and medical services for diagnostic and evaluation purposes. The most recent amendment to IDEA is P. L. 105-17, passed in 1997.

Service coordinator   - someone who acts as a coordinator of an infant's or toddler's services, working in partnership with the family and providers of special programs; service coordinators may be employed by the early intervention agency

Services/service delivery   - the services (therapies, instruction, treatment) given to a child with special needs

Special education   - see special education programs and services

Special education coordinator   - the person in charge of special education programs at the school, district, or state level

Special education programs/services   - programs, services, or specially designed instruction (offered at no cost to families) for children over 3 years old with special needs who are found eligible for such services; these include special learning methods or materials in the regular classroom, and special classes and programs if the learning or physical problems indicate this type of program

Special needs   - (as in "special needs" child) - a term used to describe a child who has disabilities or who is at risk of developing disabilities and who, therefore, requires special services or treatment in order to progress

Speech/language therapy   – a planned progam of treatment designed to improve and/or correct speech, language, and communication disabilities given by a trained speech/language pathologist (SLP)